T0328351

THE END OF KNOWLEDGE

THE END OF KNOWLEDGE

A Discourse on the Unification of Philosophy

MICHAEL DAVID LEVENSTEIN

Algora Publishing
New York

Library of Congress Cataloging-in-Publication Data —

Levenstein, Michael David.
    The end of knowledge: a discourse on the unification of philosophy /
Michael David Levenstein.
        pages cm
    ISBN 978-1-62894-021-3 (soft cover: alk. paper) — ISBN 978-1-62894-
022-0 (hard cover: alk. paper) — ISBN 978-1-62894-023-7 (ebook) 1. Ethics. 2.
Philosophy. I. Title.
    BJ41.L48 2013
    170—dc23
                            2013027257

Printed in the United States

For my Grandmother,
whose wisdom long before bore these words

"Actions are right in proportion as they tend to promote happiness; wrong as they tend to produce the reverse of happiness. By happiness is intended pleasure and the absence of pain."

"All desirable things...are desirable either for the pleasure inherent in themselves, or as a means to the promotion of pleasure and the prevention of pain."

—John Stuart Mill, *Utilitarianism*

*

"Who then is the invincible? It is he whom none of the things disturb which are independent of the will."

—Epictetus, *The Discourses*

*

"It is however, reasonable, to have perfection in our eye; that we may always advance toward it, though we know it never can be reached."

—Samuel Johnson, *The Adventurer*

*

"A wise and frugal government, which shall leave men free to regulate their own pursuits of industry and improvement, and shall not take from the mouth of labor the bread it has earned—this is the sum of good government."

— Thomas Jefferson, First Inaugural Address

"There is a natural aristocracy among men. The grounds of this are virtue and talents."

—Thomas Jefferson, Letter to John Adams

*

"Of all things the measure is man..."

—Protagoras, *Truth*

*

"From each according to his ability, to each according to his work."
—Joseph Stalin, 1936 Soviet Constitution

*

"Character is destiny."
—Heraclitus, *Fragments*

*

"Two things fill the mind with ever new and increasing admiration and awe, the more often and steadily reflection is occupied with them: the starry heaven above me and the moral law within me...I see them before me and connect them immediately with my existence."
—Immanuel Kant, *Critique of Practical Reason*

*

"Virtue is true nobility."
—Motto of Trinity College, Cambridge

TABLE OF CONTENTS

PREFACE

Philosophy as the 'Central Subject'

THE PURPOSE OF THIS BOOK is twofold. Firstly, it seeks to advance a lucid theory of moral philosophy universal in applicability and consistent in formulation, one possessive of the auxiliary allurement of concatenating previously rival and incompatible moral frameworks which may now be coherently incorporated within this grander theory. Secondly, it attempts to reveal that in the specific delineation of a grand theory of ethics, an added, perhaps more significant, lagniappe emerges: the realization that the remaining disciplines of politics, economics and aesthetics are subsumed into this narrow branch of theory, and, underpinned by a unique metaphysics and epistemology, create in the process a single yet entirely unified philosophy. In doing so, this treatise represents the culmination of my moral, and in many senses altogether philosophical, ruminations, unique in its ability to both propose a lucid moral framework for every possible sphere of human activity which subsumes all major competitors within it and to incorporate into that the remaining major branches of philosophy. In this sense, this text's ambition does not fall short of attempting an overarching theory of knowledge, and in so doing, advances a claim not to quash further debate as to solving our most enduring philosophical problems, but rather to at least provide a definitive framework in which their answers may be readily attained and clarified. I do not seek to supply responses which cater to the minutiae of life's queries, but instead the broad brushstrokes by which their elucidation may become subsequently apparent to us each as individuals. I call this system *Equiism*.

Nonetheless, my central focus is, and has always remained, ethics. For several years now, no subject has consumed my thoughts with greater longing and ferocity than that of morality—that 'first discipline within the central subject.' I use this carefully chosen phrase to connote the gravity with which I treat this branch of knowledge, in recognition of its supremacy over all other disciplines—the reason being that while philosophy may certainly prove abstruse and impractical, it nevertheless remains the most accessible and vital subject of all, for it alone dares step forward with sufficient confidence to answer that greatest of questions: How ought we live? This, a firmly *ethical* question, is the first to be asked by the thinker, and hence the highest priority for philosophers to allocate their mental resources toward solving. Only philosophy provides us the tools to forge an answer, and the required journey of our investigations encompasses a study of virtually all things related—however tangentially—to the human condition.

When confronted with the imperfect, inconsistent and trying events of life, it is only philosophy which provides a constant guide toward purpose and resolution. It is the certain fallback for a man gripped by the uncertainties of a crude world. For, it is even the man stranded on a desert island who must resort to philosophy to survive; mere sustenance and libation do not qualify as existence without contemplation and a meaning deeper than that to be had by animals. Before one can understand the nature and subsequent purpose of our existence, one cannot commence without an exploration of philosophy. Whether it is an ambition to conquer knowledge of the stars and seas or to survive sedentarily yet blissfully, one cannot learn to appreciate either lifestyle without an appeal to axiology. In devising the best means by which men should cohabitate, one cannot find hope of success without resorting to political theory—a direct extension of person-to-person ethical principles. Even the appreciation of art is meaningless without exposure to ample reflection regarding aesthetic judgment. Quite simply, we find in philosophy the beginning questions and guiding paths which seek the realization of the good life, and one confident in each of our capacities for growth and understanding that this goal may be achieved by all, provided such a course is not undertaken lightly by any, and with the warning that much contemplation and courageous action are both essential to its ultimate success.

We may wish the good life to be an easy pursuit, but reality has unfortunately provided us with no such respite. Philosophy is useless if not the benefactor of either pure intellectual joy, or the knowledge of how to better our lives in practice. It is valuable as an activity only so long as it provides a route to better living, and necessary because life is imperfect. Philosophy, in short, is the art of living well.

It is thus that man turns to philosophy, for therein are held the very seeds of his potential, cultivated fully only upon its successful and extensive navigation—a course covetous of such courage, perseverance and enlightened judgment that too few ever reach its halcyon end. Why does it require courage to be happy? Because happiness requires us to be reasonable. Why does that require courage? Because man is inherently predisposed to the unreflective, effortless and reassuring appeal of extremes. It requires discipline of will to overcome this tranquilizing destructive tendency, and in doing so, possess an inner calm requiring of no sustenance outside of confidence in the self. The courage to behave reasonably is the father of imperishable happiness; pain, exists only by permission. And, courage lives in all forms which overcome fear—in short bursts for great acts of spontaneity to the unsung and sustained presence required in toppling lesser, daily woes, and to everything in between. Let us not forget that the value of courage lies not in fearless action, but necessary action in spite of our fear. Fear of wrong is no sufficient defense; it is its own guarantor when so severe that it prohibits us from taking those risks necessary to be right. This book is an attempt to reveal that halcyon end, too often shrouded in obscurity, as one which concludes that the value of life is in the experience of pleasure, and that morality serves as the legitimate means by which we may pursue it. To know good is simple. To do good is not. It is my highest aspiration to make one these two realities, and afford a measure of ease to the latter.

A further function of this book is to recognize the importance of the disjuncture between theoretical purity and practicable reality, the latter of which is far too often disdained by scholars in their ivory towers. I have long held the pragmatic view that any worthy theory must be actionable, despite its never possibly being so inclusive or specific a guide to action that all conceivable circumstances are covered. Even a generally actionable theory exposes holes between itself and reality, and these must be bridged by 'allowances of reasonability.' As I define reason in part by an acceptance of our imperfections relative to meeting an inflexible normative standard, these allowances are essential in letting one flourish in reality, provided he remains *fundamentally* adherent to such a standard. Theory by its very nature requires internal consistency; reality provides us no such luxuries. For this reason, we must recognize that not all prescriptions shall always be followed, but we ought never to formulate ones which can never be followed. The most we can aspire to is a general framework; human judgment must fill the remaining void. No philosophy can or ought be so complete as to prevent a man from requiring personal judgment. Equally, reason permits qualification, never contradiction, whose green arc is broad enough for all men to be without excuse when knelt before their sentencer. While this may cause despair at the hands of theoreticians, I would prefer to look at this shortcoming as the only essential opportunity given each man to prove the caliber of his unique character. Nevertheless, in articulating differences between theory and practice, we must preserve as much continuity as possible; this project is especially crucial when applying normative ethical principles results in significant real-world implications ranging from political organization to the limits of State power. While we often understand ethics and politics as disparate, the two are in fact congruent; whereas the former focuses on interpersonal relationships from the psychological viewpoint of the agent himself, politics magnifies such a conception macroscopically, concentrating on agent-neutral extrapersonal behavioral prescriptions independent of any one individual perspective but as they exist *between* them, thus occupying a bird's-eye or third-person omniscient point of view. A political viewpoint is one which acts as an impartial moral judge. Ethics and politics are compatible upon recognizing that moral principles are so because of something intrinsic about them, something independent of context. Thus, what is moral between two people must be identical to what is moral amongst two thousand. Accordingly, we may understand *ethics as the study of interpersonal behavioral prescriptions actionable by the individual,*[1] and *politics as the implementation of those conditions permitting the actionability of ethics on a macroscopic level.* As we shall discover, political implementation need not diverge from nor contradict the principles of ethics, but in fact may wholly adhere to them, for prescribed behaviors and the conditions which facilitate them share identical properties and requirements, differing only in numerical scope of applicability. Hence, politics is but an extension of ethics, maximizing the good the latter seeks to a wider audience.

In this text, I aver that morality is a valuable activity because it achieves some conception of the good, because that good is inherently valuable, its own end, and that it ought be the stuff of a worthwhile life. For me, solving the eternal riddle, 'How ought we live?' is unrivalled in importance because the solution permits for us to be happy—the only indisputably good end which exists. Thinking about the nature of that good (here synonymous with pleasure in its various incarnations) lays forth certain rules regarding how it may be legitimately obtained (via means which do not contradict its experience, eliciting knowledge of lacked desert or guilt, etc.) as divined by reason. Understanding ethics is thus the key to opening the gate of happiness. Ultimately, and intuitively, whatever maximizes such good is the most pressing moral action. Because morality is simply the framework to achieve a valued end, whatever is the most prized good is also

---

1 The bulk of moral science concerns interpersonal relations, owing to the inevitable network of interdependence which typifies human social interaction. However, there is a distinct branch of ethics dedicated to intrapersonal, or self-regarding, acts. Its purpose is to recognize the importance of treating oneself as an agent equal in moral consideration to any other individual, whereby self-treatment must accordingly be understood as a highly serious and essential activity, especially in circumstances of limited social interaction, to be discussed.

the highest moral priority. While such a brief sketch of my understanding of ethics implies 'the bigger, the better' in regard to aggregating an axiological value as coincident with maximizing the moral weight of an act, such limited explanation is insufficient in defending a utilitarian framework. The problems herein prove far more complex than to be mistreated by so informal an analysis, as is to be shown.

Lastly, I pose a conception of philosophy perhaps starkly different from most of my peers. It is one both heavily deferential to the unique merits of this discipline, yet acutely aware of its distinctive shortcomings, especially as regards the uselessly esoteric (valuable only in mildest form if providing of some small intellectual pleasure for overactive thinkers). While it undoubtedly is an essential—perhaps *the* essential—activity required for the fullest *theoretical* realization of our potential, it is one nonetheless which must be ultimately abandoned for the *tangible* realization of said potential. The reason being that philosophy is no more than a guide, one which can only advise and accede regarding the ideal judgments we should make in life. It exists, like all thoughts, in ideational perfection—a vacuum immune from the deficiencies of reality, a plenum in which is filled the promise of ideality. Accordingly, it proves impossible to live purely in any sense. Human comprehension cannot escape analysis, itself conceptual model-making. And, whereas life is like the imprecise beauty of the form of poetry, the rigors of philosophy are distinctly limited, however clear, in their conclusions. Rather, the highest truth we can learn as humans is to straddle the steep crevice between the real and the ideal, and to recognize that acceptance of the former and its conditions must come before we can learn to appreciate them—something only possible via pursuit of the latter. Hence, philosophy is but a temporary Virgil, one whose recommendations must be fully and intuitively known before full life can be experienced, but one whose very submission to intuition rather than the continuous and conscious rationalization which must precede such familiarity is crucial for the full experiencing of that very life. The training wheels are required for riding, much as philosophy is for living, but neither is at their best if what should be fleeting friends decide to linger. Otherwise, life shall continue in stunted growth, relegated to a lower form of consciousness and being, one whose joys remain perpetually unripe to savor.

If any are to learn from this book, if there is anything which can or should be learnt from it, then let such wisdom percolate into the seedbed of one's unconscious and act as an obumbrated guide, but never to be forgotten that the free breath of personal judgment unentrapped by constant contemplation is but one key for bliss. Where thought is required, few men venture. No guide is all-encompassing or omnipresent, but just that— a guide for general consumption which may never replace the necessary burden and blessing of a man's character ultimately being defined by his own judgments and not those of another. Let not any philosophy constrict the bloom of our spontaneity nor its inestimable value, but let both its habitual prudence and the refreshment of good judgment serve as pillars upholding the best existence over which we may preside.

M.D. Levenstein
22 January 2011
Philadelphia

INTRODUCTION

What is Equiism?

FOR SEVEN INTENSE YEARS, I have attempted to learn what it means to lead a moral life, and in so doing, find happiness. It is a journey, as I have oft noted, which has brought to me realizations and experiences unthinkable prior to its onset, ones defined as much by the revealing extremes of human frailty as by our limitless capacity for endurance, survival and flourishing. My views have metamorphosed throughout the duration of this philosophical voyage, as much as the patterns within a kaleidoscope. But certain beliefs have remained and withstood the grinding tests of cynicism and base reality. They are few in number, but unchallengeable in import—that there exists the eternal opportunity to craft a meaningful and durable purpose to life, that it entails the pursuit of virtue, and that subsequently, the *summum bonum* that is deserved happiness may be savored by each of us.

Not for a moment have I ever been deluded into the belief that most people are inherently decent, or gravitate toward the good by virtue of some intrinsic self-guiding mechanism. Rather, for the unreflective mass, morality is a necessary procedure—

occasionally beneficial, often inconvenient—which they feel impelled to follow for both the continued functioning of society and because its precepts have been so inculcated in their minds that its departure proves psychologically untenable, if not coupled with a fear of punishment, divine or terrestrial. This is not to say that most, functionally, behave fundamentally morally (or immorally for that matter), as they are absent of requisite intent and reflection; neither do I support that religion and civic moral engineering are not vital tools toward the maintenance of social control and communitarian stability. But it is to say that the majority travels through life most unsocratically, and that despite the incommodious effort demanded by the loftier philosophical existence, it proves the unquestionably more valuable and worthwhile.

Equiism, the science of the due, is the systematic conclusion of my personal thoughts and experiences, encompassing all of the traditional disciplines of philosophy such as ethics, politics, metaphysics, epistemology and aesthetics—for each is an unavoidable facet of our existence. Holistically, Equiism understands the bulk of the philosophical agenda—including political, economic and even aesthetic questions—to reduce to ethics, itself grounded upon a unique metaphysics and epistemology, whose ultimate purpose is to lead a happy and utile life. If one had to sum up the Equiist project, it would identify that the meaning of life is to be happy and make worthy others so. Its mantra? That happiness is virtue, the fruit of reason. The purpose of this section is to introduction readers to the overarching themes of this outlook, and the consequences of its guiding principles.

Before continuing, it is useful to note the genesis of this particular system and the conditions under which it was created. Like so many raised within the last quarter-century in conditions—both material and political—of relative prosperity, I grew up with the themes of capitalism, democracy, natural rights, utilitarian calculation and the panacea of technology running through my blood as habitual understandings of reality. The thinking man however—born, I suppose, more than made (for his scarcity among presumed coequals of upbringing and circumstance implies an intrinsic rather than self-contrived identity!)—is fated never to endure the listless calm of doctrine, but destined to a life of ever-questioning and deliberative agitation. Such was my fate, often thought akin to a gilded albatross, and I expect the progenitor of my earliest cogitations. It was in particular the grave injustice of the world—and the impotent capacity of both contemporary theology and philosophy to account for or defend it—which gave rise to my own, very human, impulse, to seek to know for myself. The content of the following pages are what I have to dedicate to the world and her thoughts. I am confident of their rightness, though scarcely certain, for certainty remains too great a demand to be made of any man. Nonetheless, these are the truths which provide truth enough for me, which provide the sufficient principles for occupying in my existence more than a shallowly hedonic and amoral pedestrianism—things which provide, both great restraint and, by virtue of the aforesaid, great freedom.

Understanding Equiist thought requires locating the primacy of reason, and its unique and specific definition throughout this, and related, texts. Equiist reason is unique insofar as it is defined as 'that tool of judgment, composed of processes most reflective of the human nature, required in the formulation of ideal decisions, themselves determinable by the optimality of their consequences.' This is not synonymous with classical conceptions of reason as being interchangeable with philosophical logic. Rather, Equiism posits that reason is a tripartite method of knowledge acquisition, comprised of rational (of which intuitional, herein understood as accelerated rationalization the result of repeated use, is subset), emotional and experiential—that is, empirical—learning. Altogether, these three methods of comprehending the outside world are equally essential in the elucidation of our inherent natures and the moral laws by which we must follow for interpersonal stability and intrapersonal satisfaction. Equiism holds that reason is accessible to all, and that, however much courage is required in its implementation, its mandates are always recognizable, actionable and utility-maximizing in every situation. There is nothing concerning happiness beyond the will of the courageous. Ever may we possess the wherewithal to clutch upon that silver thread of reason, whose loosening of grasp may be made instantaneously restorable if only for the will and clarity of thought to do so, a purifying inhalation which refocuses the mind as well as the spirit. However seemingly hidden, however much courage is required to venture upon its way, the path of reason is always apparent and navigable. The distance between self-bondage and self-liberation is the courage to live reasonably. All disciplines of Equiism are informed and governed by the applications of this unique brand of reason. One cannot but believe in the infinite perfectibility of man via reason as a sustained activity, recognizing its capacity for ever-improvement despite the inability, whether collectively or individually, to achieve total perfection. To ever approach that goal however—yes, therein lies our beauty, purpose and toil.

In outlining the flavor of the Equiist oeuvre, we must first look toward the metaphysics and epistemology, collectively termed *objective materialism*, upon which the rest is based. Equiism posits that there exists an objective reality, independent of perspective and absolute in nature—analogous to the common sense understandings of modern science insofar as physical nature is the extent of tangible existence, and that it operates according to certain universalizable principles which ensure its predictability. Moreover, what is beyond the realm of empirical falsification is beyond the realm of testable, and hence scientific, knowledge. Thus, its metaphysics are materialistic. This mandates that our understandings of epistemology are colored entirely by available and comprehensible evidence, and that accordingly, all knowledge, as herein defined as *best justified belief per available evidence*,[1] is contingent and may never rise beyond the level of probabilistic hypothesis. This inevitable uncertainty is forcibly unproblematic as its ramifications are rarely visible, and since the unthinkable alternative is epistemological nihilism. Equiism posits that human certainty remains unattainable via human means, for it requires the *omnipresent*, *omniscient* and *omnitemporal* verification of the validity of information, and these correspond to a tripartite shortcoming on the part of humans: our

---

1 The traditional Platonic addition of 'truth' in defining knowledge as *justified true belief* is omitted owing to the human impossibility of corroborating any information as actual because of the abovementioned human epistemic limitations.

finite occupation of space (as opposed to existing in all places simultaneously in which to ensure the validity of a proposition), our finite comprehension capacity (*e.g.*, of external dimensions, non-visible light spectrum, etc.) and our finite chronological existence (bookended by birth and death, beyond which falsifying episodes may occur for a given proposition). Before this threshold is met, all knowledge must be accepted tentatively, though ostensibly held in widely varying degrees of confidence per corroborating evidence. Accordingly, Equiism rejects all empirically unfalsifiable forms of existence and activity as highly improbable—and hence functionally inexistent—including God(s), the human soul and miracles. Equiist epistemology further states that both reason (understood not simply as rationality but also emotional and experiential knowledge) and empirical information is critical in the development of understanding a reality ontologically independent of individual perspectives. In this regard, whereas empiricism provides us a direct and more immediate glimpse into the nature of physical reality, our limited sensory capacities must give way to rationalism, of whose function is to provide missing explanatory links, *provided they are grounded in empirically-explained, if not empirically-proven, models*. This framework, which prioritizes empiricism at its core viewing rationalism as a necessary, though secondary medium of empirically-based extrapolation, is understandably known as *synergism*.

Furthermore, the human nature is understood as one inherently self-interested and motivated, unlike that of lower animal life, by reason, complex emotion and expansive experiential learning. While it ultimately seeks its own sating, this process requires the pursuit of both short- and long-term goals, the former of which are principally physical and emotional, the latter of which are principally rational and intellectual. A central canon of Equiist doctrine is that all human impulses and desires are hedonic in nature—that is, only that which promotes the experience of pleasure is valued. Understandably, this strongly colors Equiist ethics as fiercely hedonistic and, by extension, utilitarian: whatever maximizes pleasure is the highest good. However, Equiism draws an important distinction within utilitarianism insofar as it cites personal merit, as opposed to maximal population, as the chief criterion in the allocation of utility-producing resources. In doing so, Equiist ethics—herein named *meritocratic utilitarianism*—is an innovative bridge between maintaining deontological respect for individuals whilst permitting a utilitarian calculus in situations wherein rights contradict and cannot all be simultaneously respected and/or where providing each his due in a given situation is impossible. In situations such as these, Equiism recognizes not only the moral permissibility of maximizing utility for the greatest number, but the moral imperativeness of such action. However, unlike Benthamite utilitarianism, Equiism recognizes that not all pleasures are created equal, thus adopting a Millian hierarchy of pleasures. Accordingly, not only is maximizing the number of worthy individuals an important utilitarian consideration in Equiist ethics, but so too is the maximization of higher-quality pleasures. In fact, a unique Equiist moral imperative is the prioritization of maximizing higher-quality pleasures *before* lower-quality ones, regardless of the number of individuals who may benefit from either class, assuming that the individuals affected by either class of pleasure are comparably worthy. In short, meritocratic utilitarianism is the idea that one ought maximize pleasure for the greatest number, proceeding in descending order from highest- to lowest-quality pleasures, whereby one ought not distribute lower-quality utility-producing resources prior to exhausting the distribution of higher-quality utility-producing ones.

Equiist ecopolitical theory is a direct extension of meritocratic utilitarianism, whereby economics is understood as those exchanges which normatively result in the *widest* (farthest-affecting populationally) distribution of the *highest* (quality) utility, and politics that set of social conditions under which large numbers of individuals may stably coexist per standardized codes of behavior. Equiist ecopolitical theory consists of two branches: *Retroconservatism* and *Ecopolitical Utilism*, its theory and practice, respectively. Retroconservatism articulates a new political philosophy grounded upon the tenets of what is herein described as *Social Naturalism*, or the naturalistic study of how humans organize socially. It advocates that the function of society is to benefit the individual, and that the former must accordingly seek to *conserve* its best and necessarily limited resources, most especially in the form of human capital. It holds reason as its foremost standard in both normative policy formation and implementation; moreover, retroconservatism accordingly seeks to conserve not tradition so much as the original tool of reason once bare in the natural state of social affairs and relied upon for lack of any other judgmental capacity. Retroconservatives seek a return to its reliance as opposed to the long devolved and diluted forms it has taken vis-à-vis particularistic agendas, state propaganda, political partisanship, redistributive markets and so on. Its actionable incarnation, ecopolitical utilism, is a variant of classical liberalism, named differently to distinguish its philosophical justification upon the basis of utility as opposed to natural rights or a chief respect for personal liberties. Ecopolitical utilism advocates capitalism with limited welfare programs as its foremost economic theory and an elitist-led democracy as its political theory. Its economic theory, modeled after the theory of valuation herein expressed as *Economic Naturalism*, broadly argues that the worth of objects is context-dependent as opposed to intrinsic, and extends only so far as its capacity for producing utility under given circumstances.

Equiist aesthetics, like its politics, is a subset of ethics. Art is ethics in its purest form. Equiism understands the practice of art as the highest pursuit of the ethical ideal insofar as the former aims to produce pure utility, uncorrupted by the interfering adulterants of social and introspective reality. Accordingly, its subject matter should be relevant, conceptually clear, comprehensible and elevated to the extent that it may deliver pleasure as opposed to revulsion; high art is distinguished from low art per its ability to convey higher or lower pleasures, and the efficiency with which it fulfills this aim. Whereas low art may still evoke pleasure, and be classified as art, it is nevertheless inferior to that which positively stimulates the higher aspects of the human nature—namely profound emotions and the intellect. For these reasons, Equiist aesthetics is termed *Formal Realism*, a school which emphasizes appeal to an independent objective reality but one whose subject matter should be conceptually clear and complete, though not necessarily classical in persuasion.

Whereas Equiist aesthetical or ecopolitical theories are the offspring of its ethics, Equiist psychology is rightfully the origin of its ethics, for only in the prerequisite understanding of the human nature and its behavior can one appropriately divine the code by which we should live per both our natural inclinations and capacities. The theory implicitly advanced herein, *Differential Psychology*, is an all-encompassing one which while viewing human behavior as fundamentally pleasure-seeking, deconstructs it into componential units each driven by unique motivational cognitive mechanisms. The interrelationships between these diverse mechanisms help to explain our subsequent personality, expounded in the *Conflict Theory* discussed in a former work, which broadly advocates that one's unique identity is the result of a two-step process of axiological valuation and the level of adversity encountered in the pursuit of such interests. Personality is shaped in response to the level of adversity faced in the pursuit of our wants, and the subsequent durable coping mechanisms we adopt. The psychological project of Equiism is to direct an individual toward personal satisfaction, reducing the inherent turbulence of personality formation. Hedonically speaking, it seeks to craft one's happiness as immune to disruptive externalities and the offspring of ethical behavior which itself causes subsequent knowledge of being worthy of happiness, whereby such knowledge is itself both a prerequisite for, and the purest form of, happiness itself. The end result is a man content with his moral fiber and achievements, and continuously energetic in the exploration of new hedonic projects. This last element requires an inextinguishable ambition found in the most joyous and interesting of souls, and one that Equiism lauds as the truest testament of a life savored to its utmost.

The above elements comprise the formal skeleton of Equiist thought. Before their underpinning details shall be enumerated, it is equally important to discuss the ideal Equiist attitudes as held by the individual toward his self and others; that is, his *personal outlook*. Despite its attraction to the formalized style of analytic philosophical argument, Equiism is above all a child of the Enlightenment and its foundationalism—though a long-orphaned one at that. Equiism asserts that in reason—again, not icy rationality but that method of judgment which is most reflective of the human nature and hence best equipped to promote an ideal lifestyle—is found the infinite and omnipresent capacity for self-willed happiness, that through attitudinal adaptation in the midst of even the most trying circumstances the temperate man shall overcome adversity. In this regard, the importance of a stoic disposition is crucial, as is the paired belief in the invincibility of the will, provided its bearer is of sufficient courage to wield it. Therefore, the mainstay of happiness is not material possessions or externalities. It is a state of mind. Happiness is a choice, not luck. For the Equiist, moral behavior is the means to deserving—and the prerequisite for experiencing— happiness, and that the facilitator of both such behavior and its reward is the direct result of the strength of our will. Only the moral man is happy, regardless of his circumstances. While we recognize no man is perfect, and that indeed acceptance of our intrinsic imperfection is critical to achieving happiness, it asserts the inescapability of his capacity for moral fundamentality, and that in his achievement of this goal, if not excellence itself, he, the imperfect being, becomes *humanly* perfect, fulfilling his utmost potential as determined by his obedience to reason. Acceptance means believing our thoughts and actions still entitle us to happiness.

In Equiism, I have found a beautiful and coherent framework in which to yearn and value in life, one which has provided innumerable insights and an unparalleled capacity for existential zest and fulfillment. It is not perfect, and presumably not so for it recognizes the fallibility of all men, a central virtue in their very humanity. It does not seek to provide answers for the most negligible of questions, or pettifog the minutest of pedantic philosophical disputes, but instead those which are important enough to occupy our reflections and concerns. It is the superstructure of my life's work, to be built upon by achievements as tangible as its directives provide assurance and meaning.

My labors in philosophy are not complete with this work; it is but a compilation of truths found throughout all of them— and even yet, my discoveries are not more than an approximation of truth. But still, I have found meaning, and though it be imperfectly incarnated, it is pure in form, and one I ever desire. It is the source of my happiness, my continued yen for being, and among the greatest of gifts givable man. I hope others may find such solace in its counsel as I have.

PART I: EPISTEMOLOGY

The Nature of Reason

IT IS ONLY FITTING that the lynchpin of any systematized philosophy exists in its theory of knowledge, from which all derivative disciplines must clearly be informed. Equiism is no exception, and accordingly, the most coherent path upon which to journey in its elucidation ought to begin with an exploration of the central tenets of its epistemology. In doing so, its attitudes toward not only the nature and limitations, but also the plausible applications of, its content and reason shall be discussed, and shown to apply uniformly throughout the construction of the various remaining branches of philosophy—namely, ethics, politics, aesthetics and metaphysics.

Most pressing for the Equiist epistemological agenda is the nature of reason. A term bandied about with dizzying frequency, revision and disparate meaning, it is to once more receive further edit. Reason, as Equiists see it, is that tool of judgment most reflective of the human nature, which accordingly is most apt to produce judgments resultant in optimal consequences. *In this sense, Equiist reason is synonymous with wisdom.* Immediately, this requires us to adopt a bipartite temporal understanding in the identification of what may be legitimately labeled reason, owing to its not only requisite intentional embodiment (the antecedent), but also its practical manifestation (the consequence). Whereas the latter element entails tangible utility-maximization via refinements made most ably per the instructions of experience, the initial formulation of reasonable judgments exists not in the realm of experiential learning, but in our inborn epistemic modalities: rationality and emotion. Altogether, these represent the constituent elements, or *subtypes*, of reason. Reason provides the sole means to happiness: to understand our immutable world and its laws through rationality, to accept our imperfections via experience, and to demonstrate consideration for one another via emotion. In doing so, it provides us a path to happiness which, when followed, is synonymous with the virtuous life.

Hence, we have our first colorings of reason as a tripartite tool of judgment, one principally intellectual (as to be shortly explained), comprised of rational, emotional and experiential components. The rational is fairly straightforward; in the coolness of logic and the rigors of objective argument, we find ourselves rightfully inclined to believe in the bareness and universality of human wisdom. It is, of course, in this sense with which reason has been historically most often conflated, and it is this error which is to be herein rectified. It is correct to believe that the powers of reason as a means of inevitable, universal epistemological enlightenment lay in their appeal as a fundamentally rational—that is, impartial and accessible—activity, devoid of subjective considerations. However, it is misguided to believe that for humans to behave *reasonably* is to behave solely rationally. This is a profound miscalculation, whose flawed implications are evident to even the youngest observers, myself long included. This is because reason is that mode of judgment ablest to maximize happiness by suitable appeal to the multifarious rational, experiential and emotional nature of human desire.

To behave reasonably is to exemplify the highest human ideals and discipline, for in doing so, one is entelechially exalting his fullest potential. But this is not achieved through the inhuman slavery to logic which defines automatons and whose absence distinguishes man. No, it is done by the proper obedience to the manifold nature and constituent elements we possess and which define us. While these certainly include rationality, it would be naïve treachery to dismiss the centrality of emotion to our character. Before continuing, the importance of recognizing this quality in the definition of reason is essential not only because it is truer in the understanding of ourselves and likelier leads to sensible expectations of our potential and the standards by which behavior ought be judged, but equally so in the necessary opposition to the inane premise that a man may be governed by will wholly by rationality and not his more primal—if one deign call emotion necessarily lower—urges. Such folly could not be exceeded by one in the unrealistic presumptions of man, and such excessive demands would nonetheless exhibit themselves in the colossal gulf which would soon take shape between such prescribed rationality and the shortcomings revealed by experience. Thus, we must recognize emotion to be a vital part of our essence, and accordingly, necessary in the formation of what constitutes *humanly ideal* decisions. Such, as we are to understand it, is to be herein considered the reasonable. Striking the appropriate balance between these three constitute elements of reason is no doubt the most complex task at hand, but one nevertheless required in the optimization of our decisions, whose consequences not only yield tangible hedonic benefit, but also internal psychological homoeostasis and mental calm.

Rationality and Intuition

For long, the terms 'rationality' and 'reason' have often been conflated and misunderstood as being one and the same. The etymological vagueness which has emerged regarding these words is not altogether groundless; for, it was the excesses of historical superstitious and religious casuistry which required a fortified opposition to consist virtually entirely of logic, providing no quarter for the modes of thought, such as emotion or experience, which might prove so quickly devastating to its more enlightened cause. As time has progressed however, and the baseline mode of thought more approximately and holistically rational, there ought be an important distinction between these terms. And, its profound necessity is illustrated oftentimes in life, by our reliance upon human imperfection in the exoneration of our errors; that is, to be a man governed by a pure and consistent nature, devoid of any shortcoming or deviance, is a bar far too high to which to hold anyone. Thus, whereas an automaton or computer may 'act' rationally—itself the only perfectly consistent mode of judgment—a human cannot, and acceptance of this reality and the distance we cannot close we call reason. Thus, only people may behave reasonably, because reasonableness takes into account our incapacity for total rational behavior.

But this does not mean that we cannot behave largely rationally, for in fact, we perhaps may be both able and advised to do so. In that case, we must understand what rationality is. Supplying an uncontroversial definition is difficult, but essential elements of the rational must include obedience to transitive logic and instrumental—that is, utility-maximizing—reasoning, whose characteristics necessitate universal consistency in application if under identical circumstances, and Bayesian adaptation per fluid circumstances.

Intuition, unexpectedly enough, is in fact a subset of rationality. The instinctual, automatic and suddenly clear impulses of thought which typify so many of our convictions are in fact nothing more than the subconscious application of rationality. By Equiist definition, *intuition is 'accelerated rationalization,'* the result of certain habitual rational processes, whose repeated use reduces their required effort and hence processing speed. Put another way, intuition is the tip of the sword of rationality. This means that rather than intuition being a sixth sense, it is the automatized sublimation of rational thought processes. While intuition is not as explicit in its analysis as rationalization, such heightened vagueness is unavoidable and negligible, for experience proves that its directives are virtually always as reliable as those of rationality, especially when checked independently by active rationalization. This occurs for several reasons. First, intuition is effortless or near-effortless, unlike active rationalizing, and therefore less painful or negatively utile (for all effort is, at least, weak pain). If we had to rationalize every decision, we would collapse under the omnipresent pain of thought. It is automatic decision-making, so necessary given the constant influx of problems which bombard everyday life—to exert effort on each one would be our death-knell before breakfast. Clearly, a more energy-efficient method had to evolve, and such emerged in the form that we call intuition. This can be demonstrated insofar as we are most intuitively receptive toward scenarios in which we have ample experience; novel or challenging situations beyond our immediate comprehension are immediately referred to us as unsuited toward the cursory treatment of intuition, but require undergoing the more august process of active rationalization. It is important to recognize intuition as a form of specific rational processes which are often repeated, and whose conclusions and actionable mandates are therefore quickly identifiable and known to us, as opposed to emotion, because the latter is not a *positive*—that is, originating cause for action—but a *negative* one. This means that when we understand emotion to be the cause of action X, we are really saying that X was the cause of a deficiency of rationality. As discussed, no human is capable of embodying total rational behavior, and the reason is because of our emotional nature which, acting as a natural antagonist, prevents its complete adoption. When we identify our emotions as the cause of actions, we may fail to recognize our breach of embodying rationality, but ultimately, our acts are only sensible to us—prior and subsequent to their commission—as responses of which are aimed at maximizing utility, a form of analysis requiring justifications for our actions and endemic only to rationality. Thus, emotion-driven acts are more precisely defined as deficiently-rational ones. This is not equivalent to arguing that the experience of emotion is injurious since deficiently rational; it is to say only that emotions which antecedently 'cause' actions (or more technically, 'undercut' rational causes) are suboptimal, and, to a certain extent, unavoidable.

Emotion

Emotion is the sentient and mental manifestation of the ends of rational processes. Thus, whereas rationality is a non-humanly experienced process, its edicts and effects are made qualitatively sensible to us via the prism of emotion. In fact, our very reliance upon, and glorification of the unfailing aid of rationality, owes itself to its beneficial effects *as made sensible to us only via emotion*. In short, failing our capacity to feel, we would have no need for the problem-solving potential of rationality. Such a bold claim warrants proof, and here it is with two unsuspecting examples:

John loves Jane. This emotion causes him great joy one afternoon, and accordingly, he finds himself, unthinkingly, whilst caught up in the sentiment, impelled to purchase her a necklace.

Malcolm is a perfectionist, feeling compelled to live his life perfectly rationally. He has nearly succeeded in virtually every manner he perceives this mode of thinking requires him to behave, from the way in which he organizes his bathroom linens and crafts his sentences to the route he drives to work and his uncompromising sleep schedule. No matter how arduous his attempts, however, he can never fully live up to his preconceived manner of living, finding himself always falling short of the rationalized mandates of his self-expected behavior amid outbursts of emotional frustration and exhaustion.

These may appear trifling scenarios, but they each reveal two very different and vital aspects of the interplay between rationality and emotion. The first example shows how we normally think about emotion-driven actions. We receive emotion X, and this impels us toward action Y. In short, a spontaneous emotion was the trigger for our behavior as we might understand it. This is a misconception which shall be shown to be the result of absent analysis, itself the dual product of a misunderstanding of the nature of emotion and the causality of action. Ultimately, John does not purchase the necklace for Jane simply because he loves her. This is a crude explanation regarding his action. More fully, John purchases it for her because he loves her, that emotion provides him pleasure, and, by acquiring the necklace, he shall increase or maintain an otherwise-lessening state of happiness. His rationale could be any one of a variety of possibilities, ranging from his belief that presenting the gift before Jane will increase her love for him, and hence his for her, creating a love- and pleasure-based positive feedback loop, or perhaps he shall feel better about himself, believing that this gift substantiates his being a good partner, and hence is a cause for personal pride and satisfaction. Whatever the case, *there is an underlying justification beneath the experience of emotion.* In the properly functioning mind, all emotion has a rationale. This is hugely significant because it demonstrates that emotion is not a positive cause of behavior itself, but the subsequent, consequent, quality which is governed by rationalizing processes. As one can observe, John's decision to buy the necklace appears an emotional impulse on the surface, but that emotion is itself rather the experiential manifestation of underlying rational, justificatory processes to do so. However, this is not to say that we can always *divine* the rational causes of emotion, for to do so would be extremely labor-intensive considering that qualitatively, emotion often mirrors the characteristics of intuition—that is to say, immediate reactive states to predictable phenomena. Therefore, oftentimes emotion can *functionally* be treated as a cause of behavior in itself, provided that the onset of its experience and its elicited action are sufficiently proximate and not intermediated by rationalizing or considered processes, the latter of which is the result of experiential learning. Neither life nor its wisdom is wholly reducible to words or proverbs. The imprecision and premeditation of chosen words may never wholly capture the clarity or sudden intuitiveness of our thoughts, especially those wrought by emotional impulse. The very distance between human perfection and reality is that of rationality and emotion. However, to therefore assume that the latter is the source of our flawed nature is invalid, for it is an essential part of the fabric of our identity. Something cannot be imperfect if universally existent in the ideal form; to be human is to be both rational and emotional, so that perfection exists not in the outright elimination of one part of our character, but in the appropriate balancing of the two.

What about Malcolm and his perfectionism? Again, in this example, we see the negative—that is, passive—nature of emotion as a guide to action as opposed to the positive, *action-causing* nature of rationality. However, unlike in the first example where emotion *complements* a rationalized directive (buying the necklace), in this case, emotion counteracts a rationalized directive (Malcolm repeated fails to live up to his predetermined rationalized standards). While this example still illustrates that his emotions of frustration are the result of the underlying schemes of his rationalization, it further shows that there is a disjunction between perfect rational functioning and our very human incapacity to withstand it. Understanding that the predominantly physical machinery of our constitution—from our muscles to our brain—is of only finite endurance, and the demands of rationality require neither flaw nor inconsistency, leads one to accept the inevitability of our inability to ever behave totally rationally for any sustained duration. Accordingly, while one interpretation of emotion as the nemesis and ultimate victor against any attempts to wholly embody rationality makes sense, a more nuanced view is to recognize the futility, and hence intrinsically undesirable nature, of this path (for what is beyond our nature ought never be prescriptive), and to subsequently recognize that the dual and optimal combination of these two modes of judgment (to be latter added with experiential learning) forms 'reasonable'—as opposed to purely rational or emotional—behavior.

The two types of emotions which I have thus far identified include the physical (all bodily sensations) and the psychological. While both are ultimately reduced to physicalist machinery (whether motor receptors or neurons), they differ in their *apparent origins*, the former being proximate physical causes (tactility, sight, audio, etc.), the other being mental experiences (triumph, doubt, fear, guilt, loss, etc.). This bipartite nature leads to emotion serving as the sentient and mental manifestation of the ends of rational processes. Their nature and the limitations they enforce reveal that the physical machinery which permits thought and action is not receptive to total consistency (or rationality), and hence, falls short of commonplace conceptions of perfection. The behavioral anomalies which are suboptimal, rationally- or utility-wise, are the results of emotional extremes unsustainable and intolerable. Understanding these phenomena deviant from certain rationalized predictions, and their resultant effects, individually and macroscopically, is the domain of experiential learning, as now to be addressed.

Experiential Learning

Whereas rationalism is the idea that the cosmos all the way down to human behavior might be perfectly understood in the isolated vacuum of rationality, empiricism provides for us the rival and often correct interpretation that such is simply not so. Individuals are habitually utility-minimizing—a fact as counterintuitive as one standing as upright at the South Pole as the North. Heroic men falter, and fear and panic over scrutiny rule global markets. None of these events should be theoretically predictable, but all are empirically confirmed. Man is, in actuality, a highly imperfect being, and no degree of rationalism can explain the above phenomena any more than why the Sun rises in the direction we label the 'east' each day over any other. Rather we must turn to external observations of the physical world. Clearly, there is something to be said about the necessity of experiential learning. Here, we shall endeavor to find out why this is the case, and characterize the nature of this form of knowledge.

As cursorily mentioned, experiential learning of the interpersonal realm—that is, social intelligence—is the result almost entirely of our inbuilt emotional characteristics. For example, the reason a Mr. Spock would falter at a cocktail party or an icily logical robot could not sufficiently interrelate or anticipate the behavior of humans as successfully as one of us could, is because they lack emotion as a vital motivator in the development of their behavior. For either of these two, behavior should consist only of instrumental reasoning, and be devoid of the capacity for impulsiveness, unpredictability and exhaustibility, each of which is typified by emotion-driven behavior. And yet experiential learning is not confined to the social realm, but too, the domain of science, heavily reliant upon its teachings. This is not wholly synonymous with empirical knowledge, because whereas the latter deals only with sensory evidence (and is certainly subset to experiential learning), it nonetheless does not take into account the coarser, harder-to-define expertise of practice and tricks-of-a-given-trade which can only be cultivated through the *doing* of them, rather than detachedly thinking them through.

In short, experiential learning includes heuristic shortcuts of practice, the so-called 'street-smarts' developed by learning the actual way of things, as disjoined between their prior rationalized and theoretical ideal, and the nature of their likelihood and practice in the real world. Perhaps the starkest (however sterile) example of this exists in the energy output of an engine or chemical reaction; while in theory total efficiency is theoretically possible, we understand it is not achievable in reality. Similarly, just as a man may be, at birth, endowed the potential to behave totally absent of injustice, to hold anyone to so high a standard is to inevitably guarantee his failure by virtue of an exhaustible will, and to commit the only true instance of unjust treatment at hand.

Perfection and Moral Fundamentality

Considering the above components constitute reasoned behavior, and reason alone is not only the sole route to moral behavior but also inevitably defines and causes it, then it would appear moral perfection is possible. We have before us, a means toward attaining it on paper. This is especially so considering that emotion—often seen as a detriment to moral functioning— is contained within our framework of reason, and hence unproblematic in the embodiment of moral perfection. Does this imply that perfection is realistic, and if so, mandatory?

The answer on both accounts is no. While nothing worthwhile is so difficult that it cannot be done proves a practical maxim, perfection in the sense of the absence of flaw is never possible, because it requires an inexhaustible will. Before continuing, it is vital to recognize that Equiism strongly posits the existence of a free will, whose metaphysical defense shall be argued for in the next section. Sidestepping this briefly, if we define perfection as the bipartite quality of a) the good and b) its total presence, undisturbed by inconsistency or weakness in application, then we recognize the only means by which such an end may be attained—even if via reason—is through a will of infinite endurance and one immune to fatigue. For, if such were so, the reasoned man, the good man, would always choose to behave ethically, and he would be equipped with a will which made this sufficiently easy to be possible. I argue that not only is this frightfully unrealistic (even if theoretically possible), but would in fact be an assault on our moral character, for it would be functionally equivalent to the removal of our free will. Assuming moral behavior is always desirable, and enacting it in even the harshest of milieux did not engender significant pain, there is no reason as to why we would not only pursue it, but achieve it.

Doing so however would rob us of the struggle necessary in legitimizing its value to us. In short, if morality were an easy thing to do, how might we ever know just how moral we were? A man untested by struggle is one uncertain of his moral character, and perhaps never fully worthy of the satisfaction otherwise born from moral confidence forged following adversity.

Accordingly, perfection can never be possible because of the exhaustibility of our will. While this may certainly be cause for complaint owing to the inevitable difficulties intrinsic in moral behavior, this is more than counterbalanced by the necessities of such hardship in the validation of our own commitment to morality, and the subsequent joys such knowledge brings, especially on the wings of confidence in the soundness of our sincerity in adhering to them. The will, herein defined as *the manifestation of our psychological and physical wants upon the world*, is inextricably a physicalist phenomenon. Its own potential, while infinite, is practicably not so, for it is constrained by the limitations of its physical apparatuses. I speak namely of course, of the brain as an organ and the body as a perishable organism. Subsequently, the frailty of these entities constitutes the exhaustibility of the will. Such is why, no matter how committed the mind, a pilgrim cannot expect to cross barefoot over fiery lava, much as one cannot forever endure the agonies of vicious torture. All the same, the distance between external pain and self-generated moral satisfaction is discipline of attitude, trial and error, courage and experiential adaptation toward hedonic-optimizing behaviors. Where there is no action, there is no manifestation of the will, much as omission to act is itself a distinct application of it. All action is the result of our highest want at the moment of execution. It is a fine thing to be a thinker, and a far finer thing to be a doer. For, what is beyond the will lies in the kingdom of hope—waiting for either the victims of chance or its slaves. While not practicably absolute, it is theoretically so, and capable of all within the reasonable constraints of our physical potential action, calmness resultant when we direct our will toward those sources of happiness which are within our control. Contrarily, reliance upon external sources of happiness engenders all hardship, for that beyond our control can never be a legitimate source of contentment, itself born only from the knowledge of its desert, a criterion fulfilled only via the knowledge of moral activity—to be worthy of happiness is its purest form. One ought never invest his happiness in sources external to his control such that he may never again retrieve them fully, this idea correspondent to the hierarchy of pleasures which categorizes utilities per their vulnerability to perishability when subjected to external sources of deterioration, relative to their capacity for self-maintainable preservation.

Before determining the distance between perfection and moral sufficiency, let us more closely examine the nature of extremism, of which perfection is a stark example. Extremism is *'the disproportionate allocation of resources relative to their potential for utility, resulting in the production of suboptimal utile outcomes within a given contextual frame, the result of an improper imbalance of the judgmental application of the subtypes of reason.'* Reason abhors all extremes. This implies two things: first, that extremism is corrected by a proper rebalancing of the subtypes of reason (which when properly coordinated produce utility-maximizing behavior); and second, that extremism is not preclusive of any act by virtue of said act's inherent nature (for no such inherence exists), but rather, per its disproportionate demands given a situation—that is, *extreme behavior is defined by circumstance alone.* When alternatives of equal or greater net utility exist than the one chosen, such a decision may be identified as extreme behavior, a form of immorality insofar as it produces unnecessary suffering (whether to oneself, others or both). Because logic is itself an extreme (owing to its attraction toward perfect consistency), the latter is only identifiable via emotion, the source of the frailty of our will. Extremism cannot be understood intellectually, for by its very nature it seeks a pure and theoretical perfection. Rather, an extreme is identifiable only via the disastrous consequences yielded in experience and emotional exhaustion. Understanding this phenomenon is critical as it is this alone which is at the root of all suffering and conflict in the world—whether psychological on the level of the individual, or political on the level of the nation-state. The imbalance of the constituent elements of reason causes extremism, and ultimately, immoral behavior when unchecked by the proper functioning of these subtypes. While it is impossible to completely eradicate the existence of extremism (itself an extreme form of perfection), its systematic reduction ought be the universal goal of all those interested in the maximization of happiness. There are no exceptions or areas of life in which the edicts of reason should not be binding. Similarly, extremism, defined not by innateness but the circumstantial departure from reason, is universally invalid and immoral, per its effects upon oneself and those his actions affect.

Owing to these very real limitations of the will, we must ask, if perfection is not possible, what may be defined as morally acceptable? Such begs the question of fundamentality, and the threshold it enjoins. Its study cannot be understood as a mathematical science, especially since moral fundamentality is a characteristic of the broadest context possible—one's entire life—rather than the narrow focus of a single act. Determining the moral fundamentality—that is, the overall, holistic moral acceptability rather than insufficiency—of a man, is a simple calculation: *one is fundamentally moral if he intentionally achieves more good* (in this case pleasure) *than evil* (in this case pain), and *morally neutral if he intentionally achieves as much good as evil.* This of course, is a controversial definition. For, does this imply that a man 51% moral is thus good, and a man 49% moral evil? Functionally, the answer is yes, but more accurately, no. It is simply a necessary bright line which is clearly unreceptive to quantification, but conceptually valid. Moreover, the 51% man is hardly 'good' so much as 'minimally acceptable,' much as his counterpart is 'unsatisfactory,' even if possessive of partially redeeming qualities. As for the unlikely 'morally neutral' case, such a rare instance simply illustrates that the sum total of one's deeds neither makes the world a better nor worse place, removing from its agent any sense of moral or immoral stature; such as a scenario is comparable to one in which a man was never born at all, thus worthy of neither punishment nor reward. Few singular actions are of sufficient magnitude or nature so as to overall define a man as good or wicked—and yet, some can, and do. Perfection is impossible, excellence the ideal, fundamentality minimally acceptable. Morality cannot be excluded from the hazards of unrealistic zealotry. Virtue is its own vice if extreme. We must accept all those imperfections which do not reasonably threaten the moral fundamentality of our character but whose tolerance is required in order to be happy. Likewise, in the daily exercise of our affairs, action, however imperfect, must follow contemplation, however imperfect. Indecision is ultimately fatal, and decisiveness is preferable to labored precision over the negligible.

Perhaps a greater perversity is not how this definition regimentally categorizes the good from the bad, but rather what it allows to remain placed in the former classification. I speak of those scarcely imaginable and intentionally cruel actions which, according to the above standard, may be permissible so long as a man intentionally seeks their total rectification or perhaps the completion of good acts elsewhere. For example, consider a wealthy and powerful businessman, who, by virtue of either whim or depraved sadism, enjoys kidnapping and torturing unsuspecting pedestrians late at night. So long as he provides sufficiently to charity—let us say, enough to build a hospital in the inner-city saving thousands of lives annually—is he off the hook? While the ultimate answer is yes, it is not without qualification.

First, we must realize that this example, like with all useful thought experiments, treats variables in isolation and to an extreme degree, the purpose of which is to understand the applicable scope of a given principle. In this case, we witness the sheer power and universality of the utilitarian maxim in that not only is pleasure the only moral criterion (and that no act by virtue of its alleged nature may be morally proscribed if prohibitive of a greater utile end otherwise being achieved), but that its positive creation (or at least balancing with negatively utile, or pain-producing, actions) is the sole requirement of overall moral sufficiency. Secondly, it must be realized that quantification in these matters is extremely difficult, often relatively determined between acts and pleasures along a continuum rather than absolutely fixed, and best judged only in the broadest contextual frames.

A third important feature to this definition is that while the 'fundamentally moral' man may be just barely so, there is no reason why this should come about in practice. A man is moral, like any other self-labored quality, by choice, and so because he employs reason to recognize its inherent supremacy. Accordingly, he is far likelier to attempt its maximal embodiment than its most minimal requirement. Fourthly, there is the issue of effort versus consequence. Is a man fundamentally moral who labored to be such, and yet, could not produce the consequences he desired and toiled to achieve? Must consequence or effort be the criterion for judgment? As revealed in the definition, both must be present, for good intentions do not suffice, unless they exist in such an extremely rare situation that a whole man's life's desires are systematically prevented from coming to fruition that he could only reasonably be judged upon them, rather than their success. Nowhere however, could I envision a prison so thoroughly efficient in rendering its inmates impotent.

Ultimately, the issue before us is crucial in ethics, for understanding what the will is capable of is vital in the proper delineation of the scope of our moral responsibilities and hedonic capabilities. While Equiism does not foolishly ignore variance in the capacities of different individuals' wills, it does not associate these differences to the disparate natures of the wills themselves, but rather the moral strength of character and choices made by individuals. Of course, strength of will is largely only measurable as it pertains to one's capacity for necessary suffering in the achievement of some good, whereby our varying tolerance—the result of self-discipline ultimately toward prioritizing the good before the expedient—is a function of courage. The moral and immoral differ not in the nature of their will, but rather in their self-chosen strength therein to embody it, and to what extent. No man is evil in his own eyes. To be so, would deliver to him the knowledge of his lacked desert of happiness. Only destruction may follow such realization. This is not to say however, that such a fate is inevitable, but avertable through the committed resolve of moral duty. Similarly, irrationality all too often exists only in the critiques of others; all men are endowed the infinite capacity of justifying their actions.

To conclude, is it imperfection to recognize the inherent limitations of a man relative to some predetermined boundary beyond his reach, or can perfection be defined only within the grasp of what he can reach? If, as I believe, the latter, then 'human perfection' is not an impossible concept, but exists within the realm of the reasonable rather than the certain and consistent, flawless and inexhaustible. Let it be toward this more forgiving destination we journey.

Epistemic Commensurability

It is hardly obscure why epistemology is critical in under-standing the importance of the moral propositions advanced in this text. In this section, we shall explore how the various subtypes of reason are appropriately employed only within certain fields of study, their application limited to the presence of commonly-identifiable factors between the epistemic means used, and the nature of the phenomenon being examined. This 'pairing' of means and end is referred to as *epistemic commensurability* (EC), and stands as a cornerstone of Equiist epistemology.

An example of EC in practice is how one may understand various areas of knowledge. It is inappropriate for a physicist to employ emotion or spiritual inclination in the study of the universe, simply because its available evidence strongly suggests it possesses nothing of an emotional or spiritual nature. Rather, because it exists absolutely, in perfect consistency, regularity and without contradiction, only the rigors of logic and applied rationality prove compatible in divining its true structure. Thus, he who looks up at the stars and claims to 'know God' in the midst of their beauty and overwhelming enormity is committing an error of reasoning; he is employing the wrong mode of discovery relative to his object of study.

One objection which may be leveled at this theory and process of knowledge is that it is circular; for, how are we to determine which mode of knowing is ideal unless employing both itself and comparing it with the others? That is, if looking up at the starry heavens conjures awe—an emotional phenomenon—why claim that logic is superior in its divination? Simply because logic would argue it is uniquely situated does not prove that it is. How to decide between competing claims of legitimacy regarding modes of reasoning? The simple answer is that our method is not foolproof; there are blind spots, the results of each subtype's inability to be capable of understanding all phenomena. Rather, the best and most accurate means we may employ toward the attainment of accurate information is the rotation of subtypes in the study of a given phenomenon, and the trial-and-error approach of plying each mode to each object, observing which one (or multiple) proves the best fit. Thus, by attempting each mode, we not only explore those which are most suitable, but place a check upon the information revealed by each one as to whether it confirms, denies or is unrelated to a different mode's results. Hence, whereas emotion in the study of Newtonian gravity is misplaced, so too is the application of pure logic to human relationships.

Admittedly, while the aforementioned epistemic blind spot can never be wholly eradicated—a result of our very real and overall fallibility in all things, especially the pursuit of certainty—there are what I refer to as instances of 'momentary consilience'—brief, flashing moments where one may be fully aware of the nature of a thing, either through the simultaneous employment of competing subtypes of reason or by the singular and intense focus of the one appropriate mode aimed at its object of study. Apart from these rare events however, there is little capacity for one subtype to check another, insofar as each mode is alien in regards to what types of objects it can make sense of (*e.g.,* one cannot completely justify an emotion using rationality, and vice versa). Notwithstanding this, it is advocated that intuition is the spearhead of conscious experience, followed by emotional and experiential analyses when appropriate, all of which is most defensibly buttressed by the safeguard of rational soundness, the most august of our subtypes by virtue of its consistency and objective impartiality. The nature of the mind and the circumstances under which life teaches us our greatest lessons are such that we must first fly blind, before we may see clearly. We must act as if in a state of almost constant faith, afforded only momentary and rare instances which reward that faith by confirming it. And when denied, we continue onwards, until we find that faith which is shown as true. Life cannot be reducibly analyzed to the point of certainty. In such cases, embracement of our imperfections and intuitions must compel us to still move forward, accepting those few impenetrable mysteries of life. We must leap for faith before certainty rests at our feet.

Though certainty remains beyond our grasp, high probabilistic knowledge is certainly within its reach, and necessary for pragmatic reliance in daily life. It is a great yet vital struggle to overcome our need of certainty—its pursuit is as tortuous as it is unattainable. In acceptance of this, is found great liberation—

the acceptance of imperfection. In pursuit of this humbler end, subtypes can broadly reinforce one another, or point toward which one or two is ideal in the study of a given phenomenon by virtue of its own relative incapacity for fruitful explanation. EC is a sense of compatibility of knowledge, of the due, of equity between the means of knowing and the objects which provide such knowledge. It is this sense of 'equity,' extended also into the realms of moral imperatives and soundly-reasoned aesthetical judgments, from which Equiism derives its name. Overall, this process is essential, from the development of moral propositions to the construction of a political theory, because one first requires a foundation in which methods of knowing provide as consistent, accurate and reliable knowledge upon which further hypotheses may be made as possible, ultimately ensuring the most efficient means by which we may arrive at ideal and beneficial processes of judgment.

PART II: METAPHYSICS

Introduction to Objective Materialism

THE NATURE OF ABSOLUTE REALITY, now to be eagerly discussed, could not have been done prior our investigations regarding the limits and structure of human knowledge, for metaphysics altogether is irrelevant unless comprehensible to the mind, of which can only be assured if analysis first occurs upon the latter rather than the former. Similarly, we cannot delve into the heart of Equiist ethics without first understanding the metaphysical relationship between reality and our ontological being, moral authority, autonomy and the tools available to us for ethical judgments. Thus, let us begin here with an exploration of the categories of being and their natures.

Equiism asserts that an objective reality exists, independent of phenomenological perspective and consistent in nature—compatible with common understandings of physicalism and positivism as the most efficient means of knowledge-gathering. Accordingly, what is beyond the realm of empirical falsification is beyond the realm of testable, and hence scientific, knowledge. Thus, our metaphysics is materialistic. This mandates that our understandings of epistemology are colored entirely by available and sensible evidence; thus, all knowledge, as herein defined as *best justified belief per available evidence*, is contingent and may never rise beyond the level of probabilistic belief. Accordingly, Equiism rejects all empirically unfalsifiable forms of existence and activity as highly improbable—and hence functionally inexistent—including God(s), the human soul and miracles. Equiist epistemology further states that both reason (understood not simply as rationality but also emotional and experiential knowledge) and empirical information is critical in the development of understanding a reality ontologically independent of individual conceptualizations of it. In this regard, whereas empiricism provides us a direct and more immediate glimpse into the nature of physical reality, our limited sensory capacities must give way to rationalism, of whose function is to provide missing explanatory links, *provided they are grounded in empirically-explained, if not empirically-proven, models*. Thus, reasoning is an inbuilt capacity (which can be modified per empirical evidence and refinement through experience), empirical knowledge learnt subsequently. This framework, which prioritizes empiricism at its core, viewing rationalism as a necessary, though secondary, medium of empirically-based extrapolation (despite rationality being an innate capacity, though latent if absent empirical knowledge with which to process), is understandably known as *synergism*.

Moreover, the nature of time and space is viewed distinctly from other physicalist theories which often view the two as co-existent and irreducible. Equiism posits a somewhat differing view, based both upon scientific evidence and conceptual viability. It argues that time is not itself a dimension coincident with space, itself the absence of mass and energy, but rather a function of the motion of the latter two. That is, time is merely a measure of the rate at which occupied space (itself mass and energy, since the two are inextricable and the totality of existence)—is displaced. The more accelerated and forceful the displacement, the more visible the effects of time. Consequently, time is directly proportional to temperature, and, it is herein argued, if temperature were to be reduced to absolute zero, time would also halt. Much evidence supports this view insofar as the freezing of items preserves their internal constitution with little or no measurable change. Because achieving absolute zero is impossible insofar as it would rid a particle of its energy, mass and hence existence, time, however capable of decelerating, is unidirectional and must proceed forward. To genuinely recreate a past scenario (rather than merely simulate it) in terms of time, would require the precise relocation of all relevant particles as they were during the time in question—a seeming impossibility per current technology. Similarly, time travel in the future does not exist as a distinct activity so much as the ongoing collision between particles, and their subsequent re-formation which indicates the passage of time in a forwards direction. Thus, time is not a cause, but an effect, the physical evidence of the transformative nature of particle motion.

The Equiist Position on God

Throughout my earlier writings, the Equiist attitude toward God has changed markedly. Originally, He was portrayed in a classically Abrahamic and anthropomorphized sense—as omniscient, omnipotent and perfectly moral. Later, He was conveyed as possessing all these qualities, but simultaneously distant and uninvolved in human affairs, precipitating a reverential apathy toward His existence. Now, the Equiist position as it pertains to God is one of unequivocal atheism and profound skepticism regarding the utility of theistic belief in general. All earlier positions incompatible with the following are overridden, owing to what I consider failures of reasoning in my earlier formulations regarding God, including my arguments for His existence. Central to what I consider my blunders included lapses in recognizing the feasibility of infinite physical causality and the insufficiency of available information to conclude His existence—let alone any anthropomorphic (especially moral)—nature. Hence, these views represent my most recent, and I believe final, on the matter of God.

It is important however to note that from the earliest stages of my writing, belief in God was not predicated upon mere faith, but rather the application of reason, much as was the construction of all moral frameworks. This tendency remains critical in the legitimacy of any durable philosophy, for whether one is a believer or not is independent from our capacity to access knowledge of the allegedly divine, and practice its craft. My interest in God is a largely natural one, for it is innately human to question our origins and their subsequent relationship to our nature. But moreover, vital to the historical discussions of morality has been the nature and existence of God. In researching this topic, I believe I have furthered the case for the reliance of reason in the devising of my ethical theory, including the psychological priority of becoming one's own 'utility engine'—self-reliant and the source of his own happiness. The virtue of this trait is that it not only minimizes our utile inputs or costs, but maximizes our outputs, and hence capacity for hedonic provision, or moral behavior.

While philosophy has, and quite correctly so, long turned away from the necessary link between God's existence and the legitimacy of moral law, looking instead to the objectivity afforded by reason, examining theology remains important in the excavation of new strands of epistemological, ontological and ethical knowledge, especially in the display of disparate psychological ramifications associated with whether or not a deity exists. Specifically, Equiism views the overall concept of an Abrahamic God as one which enervates the individual in several ways. These include 1) its assignation of meaning to be contained within a highly improbable afterlife, rather than in the certainty of this present one; 2) encouraging the idea that self-worth is inextricably fixed to the existence of God and independent from self-device; 3) and that God is our absolute moral judge, rather than reason, oneself and our peers. Regarding Christianity, the notion of Christ as the absolver of all sins is philosophically opposed on the basis of its eradication of moral responsibility—seen as a central feature in the legitimization of personal autonomy and human dignity.

Equiism posits that a preponderance of current scientific and philosophical evidence conclusively demonstrates the inexistence of any power higher than inert physical and biological nature, including any conception of God in popular form, including most especially any anthropomorphized variant widespread among the Abrahamic religions. It asserts that while a curse to be free insofar as one is bound with great responsibility in both the creation and desert of personal happiness—a very Sartrean idea—we are equally afforded great pleasure in the absence of a higher moral arbiter. Assuming at birth that we are neither worthy of happiness nor misery, the price required in the former's attainment—that is, overcoming our insecurities regarding the meaninglessness of the cosmos and looking no further than ourselves for purpose—seems trifling relative to the larger dividends it yields. That God is a psychological crutch for the otherwise ambulatory, and one which does not in fact aid us in walking, but rather hampers its optimal execution, is a worthy metaphor in describing those mentally reliant souls whose purpose is external to their own will and potential. A meaning self-created is nobler than a divine writ.

The Future of God

Hemingway once wrote that all thinking men were atheists. While I, nor most judiciously-tempered men, might not concur to the same extent, there is little doubt that a disproportionately large number of the examining and the educated falter when it comes to a belief in the almighty. I surmise that this epidemic lack of faith owes itself to the antipathy toward dogma and unsubstantiated claims which religion tends to exemplify, accordingly enfeebling the allegiances of those whose intellectual probity forbids that which appeals to their emotions, fear and alleged spirituality, rather than the measured suspicions of the well-bred intellect.

I envision the human race as synonymous to other species regarding the evolutionary process, and like the strongest and ablest being more likely to survive in the wild, so too are the visionaries amongst our race most likely to anticipate the future and those adapting truths which prove most effective in coping with it. I believe that atheism is one of these truths-in-waiting, the future religion of the masses. Much as the individual matures in temperament and knowledge, so too does the great multitude, though admittedly much more tardily than its most prescient scions. Accordingly, whereas human equality was once scorned, and slavery or systematic political disenfranchisement on the basis of sex permitted, or belief in the heliocentric model of our universe, there is no shortage of evolving beliefs at first lambasted but triumphantly advanced by those valiant flag-bearers of conscience and cause. I believe that in time to come, with the emergence of science further perforating the domains of doctrine, with psychology coming to explain the human beast, with philosophy providing a more fundamental and accessible guide to living well and with purpose, the widespread necessity of God—already largely weakened to an implicit presumption by most—shall fade altogether.

This is not to criticize those of faith, who not only exceed greatly in number those who lack it, but contain members which I daresay far exceed my own capacities of judgment, intelligence and grace. No pleasure should be taken in hostility toward those of belief in realms greater than our own, for to be desirous of confrontation and condemnation is hardly evidence of a refined mind. Nonetheless, ours is a firm belief that in the exchange of ideas, those of greatest evidentiary merit and utility shall prove themselves victorious, and that even those religious beliefs— which admittedly, often encourage us toward great good— should be displaced by those with equal yet different efficacies, when shown to be superior on the weight of evidence available. It is not the goal of Equiism to disprove the existence of God on the basis of rendering humanity without a savior, or depriving it of a much-needed moral center. It is to rather, in pursuit of not bare truth—but the most *useful* truth—that it finds belief in God and the implications it brings, destructive to our lifeblood and vitality, our self-reliance and proper valuing of the present and our self-responsibility for happiness and morality. That religion—albeit not theism *per se* but no doubt its extension—has proved the single most recurring origin of violence and subjugation, of epistemic retardation and castigation, from the days of Galileo to the cultivation of stem cells. No atrocities were ever committed in the name of atheism, much as no man was forbidden from heaven because sincere in his disbelief rather than his want for it. A God who could not pardon a man swayed to do good by reason rather than religion is none that ought be worshipped. Similarly, if the price of heaven on earth—that is, the total absence of inhibition in fulfilling our most personal, truest desires—is hell in the afterlife, it is worth it. For, the alternative of God otherwise requiring earthly punishment before heavenly reward, demonstrates that He would be worthy of no allegiance. For, if God were a man in that instance, we could come to no conclusion other than his being a wicked sadist.

The Existence of God

Central to the purview of metaphysics is whether or not God exists, and what impact this has on derivative matters such as man's relationship to the cosmos, himself and others. How, asks the metaphysician, is knowledge of God's existence relevant in the formulation of ethics and ontology, epistemology and even science? Before answering these latter questions, we must of course look to the evidence at hand for whether God exists, a question which itself begs the inevitable, 'What is God?'

Answering this question proves not vital in our investigations, for one is liable to bias whatever evidence he may find toward the confirmation or denial of a particular preconceived notion of God. Rather, it is more objective to analyze the neutral evidence before us, and come to conclusions, if possible, regarding His nature, after the facts stand before us. A central feature of Equiist metaphysics is the notion of epistemic commensurability—a doctrine which holds that reliable knowledge between two or more agents (which is the natural state of all knowledge, for information is always transacted between human-human or human-object) only exists when subtypes of reason—rationality (which includes intuition, or accelerated rationalization), emotion and experiential knowledge—appropriately match their targeted area of inquiry. For example, while it would be epistemologically invalid to understand planetary motion by appeal to emotion, it would not be to rely upon rationality and experiential knowledge, for astrophysics consists not only of the behaviors of predictable bodies (rationality) but also of a realm requiring observational knowledge, as outer space is often so alien from normal experience it requires some empirical grounding (experiential knowledge) in addition to pure theoretical conceptualizations. Similarly, judging the moral worth of a man purely by logic is invalid as humans are not robots, but swayed to imperfection by emotional impulses. Consequently, how do we decide which subtypes are relevant in the determination of

God's existence? Whatever they may be, we understand that in the spirit of general reason, such knowledge must be accessible by every man and not specially confined to the guru-like insights of a few. For, such exclusivity threatens epistemic legitimacy, of which history informs us often leads to the portentous misuse of such powers as wielded by those with allegedly exclusive divine wisdom.

Accordingly, of reason's subtypes—rationality, emotion and experiential knowledge—we find that emotion and experiential knowledge already appear on shaky ground, for neither proves to be universalizable. Rationality remains the sole epistemic common denominator to which all may appeal in their discovery of God's existence. Before applying rationality in answering our question, we must confront the inevitable challenge that God is not meant to be rationalized—a position which arms itself with numerous specific challenges, ranging from man's incapacity for ratiocinating the nature of God to belief in Him being a matter of faith and not argumentative proof.

These viewpoints should not be taken lightly. However, they are views which must ultimately be defeated for emotional knowledge of God—that is, instinctual, automatic comprehension of His existence or inexistence—is nonsensical. We can take a page from Hume where he correctly recognizes that any such unfalsifiable 'knowledge' might be attributed to any number of other, equally plausible factors: hallucinations, drugs, brain damage, etc. Only these causes, all seemingly negative, rival the presumed nature of divine intervention because we recognize that such an experience, whether personally had or not, would surely exist outside the spectrum of positive, normatively healthy, experiences. Not only can these experiences not be confirmed by others, and hence reliably verified, but statistics reveal that whenever they can be, all such instances are confirmed to be the result of earthbound causes such as the aforementioned— damning evidence for the likelihood of the remaining few unaccounted supposedly divine experiences. Nevertheless, their potential for being genuine cannot be wholly dismissed, and recognition of this failure to achieve certainty in matters of the divine shall become a familiar refrain. Experiential knowledge of God—broadly confined to miracles—suffers the same Achil-

les' heel of unfalsifiability, for it cannot be replicated or experientially shared. Again, while it is possible that such instances
of divine knowledge are genuine, two things are implied: 1) because of the rarity of these cases, we can ascribe them to the far
likelier earthbound causes previously cited; or, 2) willing to consider the potentiality that such knowledge of the divine is actual
yet only accessible to an extremely small minority, skepticism
ought nonetheless be adopted by the vast majority as its default
position.

If one is convinced of the argument as laid out thus far, it is
apodictic that only rationality remains as a guide accessible by
all in determining whether God exists. Accordingly, how do we
apply this rationality? It is not sensible to attempt to prove God
exists by applying its *modus* to the biological world around us;
little seems divine as opposed to wholly natural and scientifi-
cally explicable about it; the same holds true of lower animal life.
Evolutionary theory has, contrary to popular opinion, battologi-
cally defended itself against even the most ingenious of criticism,
and there does not exist a single significant challenge posed to
it which has not been explanatorily satisfied, from exaptation to
intermediate mutational change, the latter of which has shown
to be not statistically random, further legitimizing evolutionary
theory. Rationally attempting to prove God's existence by reference to biological nature is futile. Thus, we are left with only
the physical realm. Fortunately, rationality is the only reason
subtype compatible with its study (for it is without agency or
emotional capacity), thus ensuring epistemic commensurability
and hence the reliability of any conclusions gleaned. In answering whether God exists, the only viable route is a rationalistic
study of physical nature.

Though virtually certain to prove contentious, I believe, after
innumerable and labored hours of contemplation on the matter, I have excogitated a clear and defensible argument as to
why this final approach in extracting knowledge regarding God
is successful, and ultimately yields that the likelihood of His
existence is so extremely improbable, that we must conclude
pragmatically, and thus functionally, He does not exist. It is
important at this point, prior to the demonstration of the argument, that Equiist epistemology informs us that all knowledge is

uncertain by virtue of uniquely human limitations, but that despite these obstacles, highly-accurate, probabilistic knowledge is attainable and must serve as the threshold of our capacity for certainty. Much as I cannot disprove the proposition that I unconsciously adore acid rock (of which I am nonetheless fairly confident—though admittedly not certain—I do not) or locate Russell's teapot, we must operate as if these were known certainties. This revelation proves unproblematic pragmatically, for virtually all action is predicated upon an uncertainty which must ultimately be ignored in order for us to go forward in life. Whether it is crossing the street, despite the risk of being hit by a speeding, unforeseen car from around the corner to opening our front door upon return from work despite the risk of a brutal murderer waiting for us on its flipside, in life, we seem nonetheless able to thrive on the contingent and imperfect knowledge upon which all our decisions are based.

Without further ado, the argument for the inexistence of God per a rationalistic study of physical nature is as follows:

> For as long as man has roamed, there has not existed any definitive proof for the existence of a deity. Recognizing that an *argument ad ignorantiam* is fallacious reasoning, this absence of evidence must be taken as more than testament to the equal probability of both the existence and inexistence of God. Rather, the extensive claims made regarding His existence, all of which fail to prove indisputable, likely indicate the improbability of His existence.

> The existence of God is well noted for being unnecessary in the thus far scientific explanation of cosmology, the nature of physical and biological nature, along with the mechanisms which govern their behaviors. It is highly likely per the remarkable progress made by all fields of science that any matter regarding the workings of nature—which by virtue of its tangible existence must be, in all incarnations, testably empirical—is ultimately explicable per the methods of science.

Something cannot come from nothing. Therefore, owing to the laws of the conservation of energy and matter, themselves inseparable, both energy and matter have requisitely existed forever. The argument by Aquinas postulating that God's existence is necessary in order to make sense of the infinite regress problem completely disregards justifying the uniqueness of God's lacked causality. Why not need He an origin? Is it because He is conscious, for so am I, yet born from distinct cause? More fundamentally, Aquinas's argument regarding infinite regress—which ultimately reduces itself to a debate on the origins of the motion of particles, the constituents of all things—is circumvented because energy cannot ever be completely removed from a particle; if so, it would cease to exist, as well as move. Because particles always undergo slight motion, motion has existed eternally, thereby rendering the problem of infinite particle motion and infinite regress no longer problematic. This is far more plausible than the existence of an entity completely alien to observational evidence, not to mention a scenario in which physical existence flashed into being from prior nothingness—a totally inconceivable hypothesis owing to the ubiquitous evidence for required physical causality subsequent to that supposed point. If nature could be brought into being from prior nothingness, why need it be regulated by causes so rigorously since then? This scenario appears patently implausible, and, lacking necessary verisimilitude, should be functionally discounted. Owing to the extremely long duration of this causal physical chain, and its seeming likelihood to extend unabated into the future, there appears no substantive argument opposing the plausibility of this chain existing forever into the past. Arguments regarding the beginnings and ends of multiple universes are subsumed therefore, since our own universe would simply be a constituent element of broader causal processes in which larger, more inclusive physical chains of causality—such as the entire multiverse's operation itself—may exist infinitely.

The classical historical conception of God as an anthropomorphic entity is grossly incompatible with the overwhelming inequity in the world and unnecessary suffering. While there is extremely little to suggest the existence of supernatural forces, there is positive evidence *against* any notion of such a force, such as God, existing in any anthropomorphic capacity, especially one worth worshipping. Assuming He is omnipotent, omniscient and omniamorous, it requires only the most basic capacity for moral analysis to realize that His omissions regarding, or direct participation in, immoral earthly activity are unpardonable. This reprehensibility is magnified because omniscience itself, assuming perfect knowledge inherently values the good of moral action, ought be sufficient for God's action in the reduction of worldly inequity, let alone His infinite capacities of power, mercy and love. If He does possess these qualities, and continues in refrainment, His worship should not simply cease, but He ought become the object of vilification. Assuming alternatively, God exists in a Deistic capacity—as an omnipotent yet uninvolved Creator—He still ought be vilified by virtue of His omission in the prevention of unnecessary suffering. Assuming that even if a heaven existed in which the good punished wrongfully on earth might enjoy greater happiness there, the avoidable suffering caused to them on earth is still intolerable owing again, to its lacked necessity yet occurrence all the same.

Moreover, there is the issue of God's being overly-merciful in allowing any man to enjoy an infinite grace with Him in the afterlife; what man do you know personally worthy of infinite pleasure for his actions on earth? Does this imply God is not wholly just, but principally charitable? Does this imply the mediocre are provided the same rewards as the saintly? Similarly, what man deserves infinite pain for his finite evils? Is this justice, or cruelty, bringing into doubt the objectivity of God's moral judgments of men, rather than their appearance as arbitrary and imprecise.

It is often countered that the unfortunate moral imperfection of the world before us is the price of free will. This is untrue, and God, an omniscient being, would know it, just as I, the imperfect author, have been able to formulate a scenario in which it is avoidable. Envision the following: God, being omnipotent, could punish all those who commit immoral actions, yet prevent their effects from ever affecting the innocent. This could be achieved by the actions being frozen mid-execution, clearly after their conception and actionable commitment. Alternatively, the *memories* of the otherwise harmed innocents could be altered in such a way that the presence of immoral actions and their effects were registered, but were not sentiently experienced—that is, they remain emotionally-disconnected memories whereby their fault and immorality are noted, but whereby they carry no actually experienced pain. Neither scenario infringes upon free will; the former permits free will to run its course, simply nullifying its ends (similar to an unintended accident in which we are able to exercise our free will but not the desired effect), the latter involves memory alteration which preserves free will but experientially dissociates its harmful capacity upon others. Because both of these circumvent the problem of evil, but do not exist, we may only assume that a less than moral God exists. This however, is highly implausible for all the aforementioned reasons; thus, atheism proves the most likely metaphysical reality of which to adopt, for neither an anthropomorphized or deistic God seems plausible in light of the evidence afforded us.

While I find the above argument insuperable, those adopting a more deistic flair, arguing along the lines of physical causality requiring a singularity which must be causally disconnected from physical processes (and hence divine in origin), still fail to overcome this superior being taking an active role in the prevention of suffering. Thus, He is either immoral (since omission is morally unacceptable, as is to be shown) or impotent, and in both cases, unworthy of our worship. It matters little if one adopts the stark atheism of the above or the apathetic deism ('apatheism') just mentioned, the result is the same: that humans are responsible for the creation of and commitment to their own moral codes, the result of reason rather than spiritual propaganda. The ubiquity of undeserved, unnecessary suffering in the world is the surest proof of the inexistence of our God, or the existence of one not worthy of worship.

In Defense of Free Will

Quite simply, belief in free will must hinge as much on its functional necessity as for its metaphysical likelihood. Whether it is because we need to believe in its existence so as to acknowledge our very real moral autonomy or because it is the actual result of biochemical processes in the brain matters little. Free will thereby exists, if only by illusion. Equiism posits the existence of free will for several reasons, not least among them that it is perhaps the most intuitive thing in the world. Most important in the misguided nature of the free will/determinism debate is the error made by determinists in conflating the lacked ability of simultaneous action (thus creating the indeterminability of the existence of free will) as positive proof for the inexistence of free will. This is quite openly a fallacious *argument ad ignoratiam*. Herein, free will is defined as *that conscious ability to decide between alternatives and actionably pursue one option over others*. Choice, its outward form, is intent with corresponding action. In positive support for our case, free will exists by virtue of capacity for free thought prior to our actions, themselves immune from deterministic impulses by the unique biological autonomy exhibited by our brain, demonstrated by our being able to sift through a variety of options prior to taking action, usually selecting that one which maximizes our preferences. Those arguing that even such supports a case for determinism since such behavior is ultimately self-interested fall on two counts; first, they have no proof our behavior is intrinsically self-interested; secondly, if so, they cannot explain those behaviors which patently violate self-interest voluntarily (such as altruistic behavior). If such opponents claim altruism is ultimately self-interested, providing notions of gratifying martyrdom, theirs is a theory explaining all behaviors—including contradictory ones—and is hence hopelessly unfalsifiable.

Moreover, action modification can occur *media res* and in ways not necessarily previously thought out rather than those spontaneously generated, and hence demonstrative of a deterministic disjunction in which there is an effect with no clear and prior cause (that is, our decision to act in such an unexpected manner). Even more convincingly, the capacity to retrospectively envision the viable pursuit of alternative courses of action indicates one is not predestined to a single course of action, much as our ability to act astonishingly differently in very similar circumstances at different times further undercuts the determinists' case. Similarly, intent always precedes action, though only noticeable when unsublimated outside of intuitive, reflexive behaviors. Nonetheless, the probability of our intents always aligning with our manifested actions (even if our intents themselves are the result of particle determinism) is so infinitesimally small if not for free will as the explanation, that determinism is wholly preposterous. While this may not with certainty prove the existence of free will, it strongly indicates it, with no plausible offensive case being made for determinism, itself reliant upon the uncertainties of the counterfactual—for it is impossible to know at all whether one could have acted differently from the manner in which one did, as he is committed to acting in no more than one manner at a given instant. One clear example illustrative of the power of our case is a hungry man positioned equidistantly between two sources of food. Which one should he move toward? Because each decision carries with it equal expected utility, rational motivation cannot be his compelling impetus (as in a deterministic, preference-driven automaton), but rather free will; the former would be paralyzed by identical preferences, the latter not. As man is clearly able to make a decision despite this dilemma, determinism fails to provide a solution as convincing as that of our simply having free will. Additionally, physical determinism does not explain the uniqueness of autonomy. Particle motion, on any level, neither seemingly nor necessarily is related to judgment formation, especially if the latter is the result of complex, irreducible biochemical processes in the brain which result in conscious decision-making. Because we are capable of different *types* of choices—whether preference satisfaction or forced self-destructive behavior—apparently undermines the idea of particle-driven behavior since such would be governed by forces incapable of diversity in outcome (such as shown here) or originality.

Perhaps most undeniable is that while the case for free will may seem overwhelmingly likely (for certainty is beyond our reach in any matter), it remains functionally vital. Free will or its illusion is pragmatic and necessary, for reasons of moral culpability as much as belief in self-improvement. Free will is the prerequisite to moral agency, and thusly, hedonic desert. It underpins our belief that the future is the consequence of our choices. And from this capacity, we recognize the paramount value of morality is valuing how we ought to live above what is necessary to do so, that the difference between survival and living is shame. Man has no limits; thus his glory, thus his horror, and all afforded by his freedom. Conversely, if one truly believed in the edicts of determinism (and I personally know none), I cannot believe he would survive but a few days, for who feels cosmically directed to eat and sleep? Who among us feels his supposedly-voluntary actions—from jogging to preparing a lecture—are as unpremeditated as breathing? None, I daresay.

PART III: WHY BE MORAL?

WHY IS MORALITY IMPORTANT? For most of us, it is a question we have certainly asked, but not spent a great deal of time fleshing out. Rather, we have most likely vaguely entertained notions of moral nihilism—the doctrine that objective moral truth does not exist—but yarely dismiss such ideas not so much because they are indefensible, but because those mores with which we have been inculcated from the earliest age refuse the possibility of even considering the merits of such fringe and potentially-condemnable ideas. As a student of philosophy, I can assert that the more one comes to 'know'—if so hubristic a claim can be made by anyone—the less one becomes *certain* of the supremacy of his beliefs. Such has indubitably been evident in my own case, where over the space of but seven years, my philosophical views have changed markedly, though admittedly, rarely ever radically. Nonetheless, what has persisted with the same fiery intensity has been my quest for knowledge, for truth and for understanding what constitutes the good life. This voyage has been one of discovery, of passion, of bitter intellectual trepidation, anguish and ultimately, self-satisfaction. Many claim that this trajectory is necessary to ultimately attain bliss, for its cognizance is sharpened only by knowledge of its antithesis—a claim I sincerely refute. Nevertheless, I have reached what I presently consider a final phase in the maturity of my ideas, and one which lends a certain subtlety and refinement to a previously-coarser comprehension of the subject at hand, a refinement which deserves, for any deeming my thoughts worthy of consideration in the first place, to be articulated before such gracious readers.

My task in this work is to consolidate, clarify and characterize divergent moral sentiments, and upon such study, to present a unified theory of ethics which transcends these seemingly-incompatible perspectives and yet successfully incorporates key elements of each, all the while satisfying the utmost burden of all—that of reason. Toward achieving this goal, we realize we are beyond the realm of still asking *why* morality is important, and instead attempting to identify *what* is moral. Because our threshold of theoretical plausibility is *reason*, its nature and role as an intellectual tool necessary in understanding ethics shall be discussed, relying heavily upon my previous understanding of these matters.[1] Nonetheless, these objectives are to be fulfilled later; this introduction is to serve as a prerequisite discussion necessary in understanding why the task before us is one in fact worth undertaking.

Why then, is morality important? Why have I, a fledgling young man in the bloom of youth and carefree days, devoted the last seven years of my life to its intense scrutiny—the distinct source of much personal melancholy? The reason is less than ob-

---

1 Essentially, reason as I articulate it previously and throughout this text (including with such terms as 'reasonable,' 'reasonably,' 'reasonableness,' etc.), is that method of judgment which best reflects an accurate assessment of human nature. It entails a tripartite composition of *rational* (of which a subset is intuitive judgment, or 'accelerated rationalizations' whose familiarity leads to their becoming second-natured and automatic), *experiential* (learning from experience and empirical reality, particularly of the schism between theory and the reality of practice) and *emotional* understandings of the world around us acting in coordination with one another—simultaneously (bi-jointly or tri-jointly) or less often, singularly, and in either case, in varying degrees depending upon the circumstances. This understanding of reason and its constitutive elements, or subtypes, offers a practical and actionable framework in which decisions can consistently afford us, both externally and psychologically, the optimal sustainable existential condition (not to be mistaken for happiness at *every* moment but rather the greatest amount experienceable [intellectually, emotionally, somatically, etc.—in all possible human forms] in the broadest contextual frames).

vious, and at times has been what I considered no more than a personal prejudice—the disposition of my particular intellect and nothing deeper. Specific personal circumstances might have indeed catalyzed my valuing ethics above other subjects, though in the subsequent cases of reason and rationalization serving as slave to these initial passions, let us not forget that upon their investigations independent justifications for the supremacy of this topic have not serendipitously, but purposefully, emerged.

Pleasure, Pain, Happiness and Utility

Of note, while *happiness refers to a sustainable outlook or way of being, pleasure more often refers to temporary instances of gratification.* Whereas there exist at least three types of pleasure (physical, emotional and intellectual) which may occur singularly or in any combination with one another (either bi-jointly or tri-jointly), happiness refers to an existential state generally comprised of all three *usually coexisting*—though it may reflect differing quantities of each pleasure (including the temporary absence of any given one or more) at any given *instant* in time. Before continuing, it is extremely important that operational definitions be accorded to pleasure and pain. *Pleasure is any experienceable comfort; pain is any experienceable discomfort.* The comfort/discomfort experienced must be the result of the satisfaction/dissatisfaction of *reasonable* preferences. Each of course, exists qualitatively along a continuum of varying intensities, as do their typologies—namely intellectual, physical and emotional. Thus, pain and pleasure can be thought of existing not upon exclusive scales, but a continuous one; imagine a number line in which all positive values represent pleasure (of any typology), the zero value represents sentient neutrality and all negative values represent pain (of any typology). For this reason, an increase/decrease in pleasure constitutes a decrease/increase in pain, and vice versa. *Utility refers, either to the probability of pleasure, its quality and quantity, in uncertain future circumstances, or to the known quantities and qualities of pleasure in past and present circumstances.* It is the sating of reasonable preference satisfaction, legitimized so long as not unduly infringing upon the preferences of others being satisfied. Despite the important distinctions between these terms, for the purposes of connotative ease and only when such distinctions are not pertinent to the subject at hand, the terms pleasure, happiness and utility may be used interchangeably. No confusion shall emerge from the bifurcated definition of utility offered, for either of its two meanings shall be known depending on the contextual usage.

Before continuing on this line of thought, let us examine more fully the supremacy of happiness. Happiness is the *only* end which is sought for its own sake and experience. Not only is this definitional, but it is true experientially. No doubt, this claim is highly controversial. After all, it unabashedly reduces the whole of moral axiology into a single value worth pursuing. Clearly, it has to be rigorously defended before we can continue, for the bulk of what remains is predicated upon this premise.

It is largely axiomatic that happiness or pleasure is its own good. Its diverse manifestations—from the intellectual (*e.g.*, problem-solving) to the emotional (*e.g.*, as found in relationships) to the physical (*e.g.*, sex or exercise)—reveal its compatibility with each of the subtypes of reason (intellectual pleasure matches with rationality and experientiality [*e.g.*, satisfaction gleaned from practice making perfect in a given activity, such as piano-playing], emotional pleasure matches with emotion and physical pleasure with experientiality [for sentient *experience* is a prerequisite to all physical sensation]), thus further legitimizing its basis for our axiological framework. For, what compels us to seek the love of another over loneliness, aspire to professional eminence, gain wealth or soak in a hot bath? The immediate or eventual aim in each of these cases is the attainment and experience of pleasure. This by itself is relatively uncontroversial; rather, the proposition that pleasure is the *only* worthwhile moral value is contentious. To this I say, but one thing: think and think, live and observe, and no other value worth pursuit, however indirectly sought, shall exist independent of this category. It simply is all that we value, all that makes life worth living. Intentionally achieved pleasure is the only good, intentionally achieved pain the only evil. Pleasure and pain constitute inherent good and evil, respectively, not because they possess intrinsic moral properties, but because their actionable manifestations appeal to categories of being fundamentally valued and disvalued by humans. Moral propositions exist only subsequent to this natural fact, insofar as one intentionally pursues and achieves either the former or the latter end. As no act is devoid of producing either pleasure or pain, however much in the slightest degree, and because either state of being is intimately bound to the nature of good or evil, there is no issue not ultimately made to be a moral one.

Moral Axiology: Autonomy and Rights

What determines a moral value? Why should we even take for granted that pleasure is, not so much its own good (that remains fairly obvious), but that it is a *moral* good? In other words, how are we to evade being cut by Hume's guillotine? The explicit and underpinning axiology throughout this text and much of my earlier work consists of recognizing that pleasure is its own natural good (it 'is' inherently desirable). Morality, as I understand it, involves constructing those rules which attempt to benefit individuals in their dealings with one another, rather than Nature[1] (which, owing to its incapacity for intent or agency, is amoral). What confers such benefit however? The answer is that which we are reasonably prone to enjoying, either naturally (as in raw physical or emotional pleasures) or through education (such as the fine arts). Accordingly, morality serves as a means of achieving that which we are to value—either naturally or through conditioning—though it is important to note that while this conditioning can *bend* natural predilections, it cannot break them or unreasonably stretch them; in other words, whatever we are to ultimately find pleasing, exists within a predetermined green arc reflective of a universal and fundamental human nature. Our nature is the blueprint by which we construct a meaningful and valued life, and moral considerations cannot be made in isolation from a deep familiarity with the human nature and those pursuits it gravitates toward. Thus, ought *does* follow is, because it is rational to pursue only what one is programmed to seek— whether by nature or inculcated choice matters not, for pleasure

---

1 The issue of animal rights and their moral treatment shall be addressed later. What is broadly referred to here by 'Nature' is its non-biological constituents: rocks, rivers, physical landscapes and all other non-sentient components.

is of both these realms. Succinctly, *morality lays the rules (a means) by which we can legitimately attain what is inherently valued (the end)*.

Following this, we can deduce that pleasure—a quality we value—is one of the ends which morality serves to afford us, the latter acting as a regulatory bridge between the desired ends of our behavior and the acceptable process by which we execute our will. Using this particular axiology, we can proceed to the earlier task of specifying why pleasure is the lone value we should pursue. Pleasure is of a wide variety of forms: it is cerebral, emotional, carnal. It exists in activities as diverse as philosophizing, playing chamber music, embracing a child, watching a football match and using illicit drugs. For this reason, we must understand pleasure as an extremely diverse and far-reaching phenomenon—let it not be misrepresented as a purely bodily or even sensory delight. With this in mind, let us consider other common axiological values, and how they compare with pleasure. This step is crucial, for what shall be shown is that these other values are in fact either deceptively misguided or subtle manifestations of pleasure itself, and for the sake of simplicity and clarity, it is best to reduce all such values to their one commonality.

Autonomy is often cited as the chief rival to pleasure as a fundamental moral value. So lauded is it that it serves as the bedrock of libertarian and many deontological understandings of morality, in which each cites human freedom as not only an inherently-valuable commodity, but moreover the lynchpin of our metaphysical dignity. This understanding is problematic for a variety of reasons, chief among them that it implicates things which are not substantiated as might first be thought. I refer here namely to the metaphysicality of dignity. For autonomists, morality is more than a set of impersonal rules we are to follow as if gears operating within a larger societal machine. Rather, each individual is of inextinguishable value, and constitutes his own end. In this regard, he exists as a non-negotiable entity of whose rights may never be permissibly violated. For them and natural rights advocates, morality serves a less practical but purer function: respect for the sanctity of the individual. In order to justify their claims, natural rights advocates will argue that reason permits us an understanding of the individual as a distinct entity by virtue of his separation of consciousness, and accordingly, that he exists naturally as his own end. To use another as a means toward self-interest or a greater, collective good, is thus to pervert nature and act immorally. All such understandings must inescapably view human beings as possessive of some intangible dignity or value. However, let us recall that the lowest common denominator in philosophical dialogue must be reason as opposed to religious or divine knowledge, for we can only judge the merits of an argument by its relationship to corroboration via our capacities of intellect and sense. Accordingly, human dignity as a criterion justifying the moral respect of oneself and others fails to meet the threshold of reason-based plausibility, for it is not one readily apparent either through observation or analysis. Dignity cannot be uncontroversially defined, nor empirically measured. Simply, there is no way to tell if it even exists, for, if it did, a human must possess some 'unseen holiness'; otherwise, there must exist logically certain circumstances under which his 'rights' may be violated. And, if dignity is even a sensible concept, it does not lie in the sanctity of life itself, but rather in the extent of its experience of earned pleasures.

In addition to dignity, there is the issue of rights themselves, and whether they actually exist. For autonomists, they are natural or supernaturally-endowed, and exist as inherent to the human being; for the hedonism prescribed here, such rights do not exist objectively in physical reality, nor within or surrounding the human being. They cannot be metaphysically identified. Appeals to the nature of the human as a justification for their existence fail because they require second-order value ascriptions. The statement 'because one exists as an autonomous end by virtue of a separate consciousness, he therefore has the right to act in the absence of coercion' is not problematic because 'is' cannot overcome the is-ought obstacle (for even the pursuit of pleasure is an 'ought' to be pursued because of its inherently-valuable nature as an 'is'), but because *rights cannot be identified as distinctly existent physically, metaphysically or ontologically.* Any creation of them requires a departure from what our senses reveal as a rightless world, much as it requires a contrivance of reason independent from objective reality. Unlike pleasure (an inherently valuable end sought by all humans), rights do not pass the axiological litmus test of proving universally sought after when compared with pleasure itself. For, as here articulated, the most basic function of rights is to secure those conditions under which one can best flourish or at the very least be uncoerced, so that, pursuant to this, one may freely seek pleasure. In other words, rights are merely a useful, efficient means of obtaining a more fundamental value: pleasure. Rights therefore, like laws, are an example of rule utilitarianism. Their necessity exists insofar as they are required for the stable functioning of society, itself necessary to permit the highest actualization—and hence, highest pleasures—being accessible to man, from the social and intellectual to the interpersonally emotional.

For the hedonist, pleasure is defensible because it is inherently sought after; toward it is aimed the full thrust of the human psychology. Rights however, do not meet this threshold of universalizability or intensity of demand; they are not as appealing as, nor sought as powerfully, as pleasure itself, whatever its form. There is nothing intangible about pleasure; it is immediately apparent and empirically verifiable; it clearly exists as part of the fabric of human motivation. Thus, we come across the first key difference between deontologists and consequentialists—whereas the former believe there is something inherently good in a moral rule itself (thus mandating that it be respected), the consequentialist looks only to the consequences of an action to determine its moral content. Thus, what is moral is not that which is *inherent* to some fixed principle (for this would require a metaphysics which is not readily discernible to the human mind or reason itself, and must thus be dismissed), but that which is palpable and desirable within a particular set of circumstances. The only quality of this sort which is universally valid is pleasure, because it does not rely on any means of understanding beyond that which is tangibly experiential or observable. It does not require distorted metaphysical conceptions of the human being, nor ascribe to him duties or rights which, in the case of the deontologists, must be intellectually contrived.

Let us go further however, in dismissing the arguments of the opposition, especially regarding the desirability of human autonomy. In order to do so, I would like to cite the oft-noted 'Experience Machine' thought experiment of libertarian philosopher Robert Nozick, in which he argues that given the opportunity of being connected to an advanced machine capable of perfectly replicating all sensations—including desired pleasurable ones—whereby the cost of doing so would be the voluntary and permanent forfeiture of personal autonomy, most individuals would decide against being connected. For Nozick and others, there is great value to the 'realness' of life, even if that mandates the experience of frustration and pain, because autonomy is inherently valuable, in addition to serving as a prerequisite for moral agency. While autonomy is no doubt crucial to moral agency, the assumed value of such autonomy in and of itself is misguided.

Let us assume that humans are endowed with autonomy—the capacity for self-determined action in the face of potential alternatives. Admittedly, we may argue that there is great value in this ability; it is what separates us from predominantly instinct-driven animals and provides us the capacity for reason, the richness of individuality and what many think of as an 'authenticity of self.' All of these arguments are plausible, and the latter statements seem intuitively obvious. That however, does not address the more pressing concern of both the ultimate value and function of autonomy. *What is autonomy good for?* This question presupposes that autonomy existing just for itself is unsatisfactory (unlike with pleasure, its own and complete good). Is this the case? Well, consider this: imagine a man is granted full freedom of thought and action, and yet his life is marked by more misery than happiness—is such a life worth living? Is the authenticity of being a homeless beggar, crippled by hunger, valuable? Or a wealthy industrialist tormented by depression? How about the lifestyle of a perfectly average man, suffering from no ailments or hardship, but simply bored of existence? This question draws into sharp relief the actual value of autonomy, for, beyond serving as a means to an end, where is its value? What benefit do we actually glean from merely the *capacity* for free action—the very definition of autonomy?

The answer is surprisingly little, if any. Instead, we value autonomy because, in light of there existing no such thing as an Experience Machine, we must confine ourselves to pursue happiness by our own devices, through the mechanism of autonomy.

In other words, though it would be ideal to have our pleasures delivered to us and without the effort of moral behavior (as through the Machine), failing that, we have to actively pursue them ourselves through self-initiated action (via autonomy). Life has no inherent meaning. Its highest function exists in the experience of pleasure, the only intrinsic good. The regulation of those behaviors concerned with pleasure is called morality and inextricably bound with the pursuit and enjoyment of the good life. But, how can we make the assertion that we value autonomy only for the pursuit of pleasure? Well, consider this: we do not seek autonomy for its own sake, unlike pleasure. Autonomy is not pursued as an end; it is merely the means toward something else. There is no value in the *potential* to do something; *value is meaningful only if tangibly achieved or personally experienced.* This last statement is critical; nothing can have value which is not somehow prone to sentience or experience, for otherwise, it has no meaning to us qualitatively whatsoever. How can one value what one cannot sense or understand? Accepting this definition of value will later serve to identify much misguided logic within the deontological tradition regarding its placing rules above consequences, whereby valuing the former when absent of all experienceability shall prove invalid when there exist other theories which dissimilarly *always* provide the capacity for pleasurable sentience via the performing of a given action or its result. Likewise, it discounts all theories of moral value not based upon action which produces either in their very performance and/or result pleasurable sentience; hence, already we have implicated that consequentialism is the only valid form of moral theory, though this statement requires great qualification and does not discount much deontological thinking (but in fact unifies it), as shall later be shown. Also to be addressed is what type of consequentialist thinking is most valid, during which the merits of utilitarianism, egoism, altruism and other brands shall be debated, according to rational and axiological lines.

In brief summary, we can understand autonomy as an empty pursuit, for its value is not self-contained. Rather, it is valuable only because it is instrumental in achieving another value, that being pleasure. There is no rational application of autonomy if not ultimately for the purposes of attaining pleasure. The value of life itself is in the experience of this essence, whose study and pursuit is the entire province of moral science. Autonomy has no value in and of itself, but rather constitutes a prerequisite to moral agency, and thus, hedonic desert. The hedonically inefficient nature of our world therefore requires free will as a benchmark of the rewards or punishments owed us, though one cannot but realize that since morality is but a means to the end of deserving pleasure, would not a superior world exist in the form of one in which pleasure—the only good—was delivered without the complications or efforts endemic to freedom or moral effort? The oft-invoked authenticity of self is only valuable if such an existence is a pleasurable one, therefore indicating that autonomist morality ultimately collapses into a hedonic axiology. If one accepts this argument, then Nozick appears incorrect in thinking that one would not willingly accept pleasure freely provided by an Experience Machine (or that, by extension, one would not be morally compelled to supersede the autonomies of others in order to connect them too, regardless of their misguided protestations, to the Machine, since maximizing pleasure, including that of others, is the only good), especially since it is done so with 'minimal costs' to the individual.[1] To think more clearly about this issue, imagine we were born as a subject within the Experience Machine. In such a case, if offered autonomy with the guarantee of less pleasure, how many would opt for that? I would imagine few, if any, for those in possession of pleasure appear rather jealous of its continued experience. What then, would prompt Nozick, and admittedly so many others, to opt for autonomy over pleasure? Though the answer is not obvious, it is most likely a combination of not fully exhausting reason to

---

1 'Minimal costs' refer to the Experience Machine providing pleasure without effort required by the individual, compared to the individual who, granted with autonomy, would have to effortfully pursue such pleasure. As experience tells us, such pursuit would not be perfectly efficient in hedonic terms, meaning that total pleasure could never be had, but that frustration and pain would be accompanied with it. Because autonomy has been shown to have no value in and of itself, while pleasure remains the only value we are universally and inherently drawn to as its own end, the fact that autonomy has higher costs (in terms of enduring pain) than the Experience Machine (which provides pleasure without limit or cost) strongly suggests that any rational agent would willingly forfeit valueless autonomy for limitlessly valuable pleasure.

its furthest conclusions, intuitive fears about the forfeiture of autonomy in light of the unknown rather than maintaining a *status quo* bias and even entrenched religious inculcations, however allegedly ignored, which traditionally sanctify the dignity accordant with human freedom. Of note however, is the understanding that the Machine in question can *perfectly* simulate any human experience, and that once connected, one is unaware he is so.[1] Thus, any fears regarding the simple unthinkability of surrendering the very quality which typifies the human experi-

---

1 Intuitively, we may think of the Experience Machine as replicating only physical, and not intellectual and emotional pleasures (though the latter would be included). This is because we tend to view physical pleasures as requiring the least proactivity on our part, which instead can be passively enjoyed. Relative to intellectual and emotional pleasures, this seems somewhat true; for example, a massage provides pleasure while one remains inactive. Such is not the case with other pleasures however; for instance, to glean the durable intellectual pleasures of an Aristotle would certainly entail active engagement [the exercise of autonomy] (not to mention a few headaches from overthinking along the way), much as any relationship in which there exists a bilateral emotional affection for the other partner—such requires proactivity on the part of the individual. This leads us to two realizations. First, that *all* pleasures require active engagement to some level, though it varies; even physical pleasures require the mental willingness to experience them (*e.g.*, one cannot enjoy a massage unless he clears his mind to do so, much as one cannot enjoy sex unless an enthused participant). While intellectual and emotional pleasures may require more effort [and the exercise of personal autonomy], all still require involvement. Second, it appears that under ordinary circumstances, autonomy—which provides us the capacity for self-initiated proactivity in pursuing each of these pleasures—is crucial, especially for higher pleasures since they require greater effort to attain, and hence, greater amounts of self-initiated and sustained activity—only possible if autonomy first exists to make any action at all possible in the first place. I am not refuting this. Rather, we must understand autonomy as part of the fabric of human nature—it is the only means by which we can pursue our one objectively valued end: pleasure. Hence, autonomy itself has no value unless capable of attaining this end; if any machine could perfectly simulate one form (or all forms) of this end while eliminating a pleasureless means (or at times pleasure-costing [hence, painful] medium, by virtue of its oft-required invested effort [as with deep thought]), it is reasonable to connect oneself to it, especially in the parenthetical case of avoiding pain. For, in the first case it is rationally preferable to maximize happiness over a non-pleasure producing activity (even if absent of pain), and certainly so to pursue a pleasure-producing end over one entailing pain, as in the second case. Hence, the Nozick thought experiment reveals to us the opposite of its desired effect: the universal and sole supremacy of pleasure as a moral value.

ence—capacity for thought and action—are upon closer, braver and less dogmatic examination, ungrounded. For, the Machine does not provide mere simulacra, but a virtual world indistinguishable from external reality via experiences which define our conception of the latter.

I cannot justify the superiority of our present reality over one in which universal happiness was achievable, even if at the cost of the absence of individual agency and moral desert. For, in recognizing happiness to be the only good, the value of freedom and virtue is but an inescapable and necessary delusion, one in which we must be resigned to accept with stoic grace in the absence of no better alternative. In this sense, stoicism is the useful self-delusion of appreciating the bearable as the otherwise unattainably desirable. Imagining pleasure to be limitlessly available in some other world, morality becomes an obsolete requirement in separating the worthy from the unworthy, since utility is no longer a scarce commodity to be rationed per individual merit. All may be happy without the efforts of autonomy, for its existence, however authenticating, inevitably leads to imperfection and the birth of sorrow. Such though, is not our world, and hence, the practical necessity of valuing autonomy and ethical behavior.

Toward a similar vein, people often speak of the unattainability of perfection as a virtue—that through our imperfection, we learn, we somehow grow. This is patently untrue. There is no benefit in a flawed existence relative to a flawless one, but it is our existential misfortune and nature which makes the latter impossible. Rather than contriving an argument demonstrating the imperfect life to be superior, we must confront reality, recognizing our highest ambition to approach perfection through ceaseless obedience to reason and its subsequent directives toward happiness. We shall never be wholly able to fulfill this dream, but our degree of success in this endeavor is the metric of the moral value of our life.

Lastly, there is the question of other moral values, apart from autonomy and pleasure. Are any of these valid? Though it is impossible to list all possible candidates, among the more common include such things as love, compassion, mercy, justice, truth, loyalty, respect for traditional culture-specific values, spirituality, faith and respect for the moral worth of one's 'soul.' Such values are problematic for two reasons: firstly, they are empirically unverifiable, not necessarily applicable to every person or are concepts relative from society to society; secondly, they are reliant more upon spiritual faith than reason, thereby making them ineligible as acceptable moral values. This is, in addition to their oracular, relative and uncertain nature, because reason alone serves as the only sufficient lowest common denominator in discussions pertaining to ethics. Anyone claiming a factor other than reason is key in the formation of proper moral judgments must rely upon exclusivity of information and experience not accessible to all others (*i.e.*, those of a different religion, culture, etc.). This sets a dangerous precedent for moral imperialism absent from considerations of reason—a piercing intellectual tool common to all rational agents. Duly, reason—as composed of its constitutive rational, emotional and experiential elements—informs us that of all the values appropriate for moral consideration, only pleasure passes its threshold of plausibility. Lastly, certain of these values, such as love or mercy, can be understood as valuable solely because of their pleasure-producing quality (hence collapsing into a hedonic axiology).

Treatment of Rights

As discussed earlier, rights are neither natural nor inborn, but the contrivance of man and his need to develop a common system of interpersonal respect which makes the development and stable maintenance of society possible. Only in extreme situations of competing interests, all of which are incapable of satisfaction or respect, may and must rights be violated, in part, to permit their partial respect, rather than their complete disregard. Accordingly, at best, rights are examples of rule utilitarianism, and as such, merely utile rules. Act utilitarian calculations should be undertaken only when forced choice exists prohibiting the implementation of deontological imperatives or utile rules, or whereby their implementation is counterproductively costly to their original purpose for maximizing utility on a general basis in cases of exceptionally high stakes.

Rights are the glue which holds society together. A man need know only his rights and duties in order to live successfully in society. However, when external forces so great lurk as to deny the continued existence of the very framework which permits the survival of those rights, the latter must be compromised so as to ensure their flourishing at a later point in time. As a general rule, no threat is so existential to a society or state that rights need be abolished, either wholly or partially, and often, the best offense against social and warring forces is to reaffirm the rights of the citizenry so as to instill knowledge of the good and a purpose for their common defense. For, a people with lives without rights, and hence lives not worth fighting for, are unlikely to respond to the clarion call for the defense of their betraying society. However, in truly exceptional circumstances—in which the framework permitting rights is fundamentally threatened—and where such actions as conscription or torture require the partial disenfranchisement of the autonomy or welfare of few, such practices are simply unavoidable.

Hierarchy of Pleasures

Now that we have come this far in articulating why pleasure remains the supreme moral value, we must consider if, owing to the diversity of pleasures which exists, they differ in terms of axiological and moral priority. As defended here, the answer is yes, in the following order of descending value: intellectual, emotional and physical pleasure. Briefly (for this hierarchy shall be expanded upon later), intellectual pleasures take priority *ceteris paribus* (that is, assuming that each pleasure exists in equal measure and accessibility, for otherwise, scarcity of a lower pleasure can render its superior value over a higher pleasure in particular circumstances) for they are the most enduring, durable and self-controllable. This is because they involve the most inextricable aspect of the human persona—our attitudes and way of interpreting the world around us, which includes our capacity for adopting a utility-maximizing outlook across even a broad spectrum of possible circumstances. Because intellectual pleasures involve the internalization of knowledge which lends itself to the creation of personality-forming attitudinal perspectives (and ideally positive, happiness-affirming ones), they remain fundamental to our very being and largely independent of ephemeral external circumstances, whether beneficial or deleterious, but rather firmly within *our* omnipresent control. What exists most within our control must sensibly be the most prioritized bastion of our happiness, for it alone serves as an incubator in experiencing happiness. Our intellectual pleasures define our personalities, and are thus inextricable from our very existence. Knowledge is good only as a pleasurable end in itself as a manifestation of the intellect, or as a means toward that end elsewhere. Emotional pleasures, which almost invariably involve social interaction (on a fraternal or familial level), are for this very reason less enduring than intellectual pleasures because they are dependent upon the existence of others (and hence subject to the potentially-changing behaviors of such others, just like any external circumstances beyond one's control), as evidenced especially in the case of love (a possible exception which surmounts intellectual pleasures).[1] Nonetheless, they prove more

---

1 Emotional pleasures can persist (and in certain cases, especially with strong forms of interpersonal love, prove stronger and more valuable to the individual than intellectual pleasures) in the absence of others insofar as they can be elicited by memories of such others. As just noted, there are instances where emotional pleasures prove strongest in contributing to overall happiness, though despite the abundance of claims to this effect, they should be treated with caution for the aforementioned articulated reasons which suggest that it is in fact intellectual pleasures which predominate in the maintenance of a sustainable happiness, even if many would consider this claim to be disconcertingly dispassionate, especially regarding the extent to which significant others play in crafting individual happiness. This is a misguided view however, for often an intellectual attitude is critical in augmenting and clarifying the very role emotion plays in how much we value others, rather than serving as a device which belittles it. It is often claimed that love is the greatest of all human experiences, perhaps the only one which validates our existence. This is dangerously untrue. Whilst love is certainly intense, and powerful, it is not what should be our highest priority in life, for ultimately, when unrestrained, it leads to the forfeiture of duty, the vulnerability of the soul to be placed in the hands of another. To wrest control away from ourselves and what we value, and provide willingly such bounty to another, is to sacrifice the only thing which may never permissibly be sacrificed: our very salvation. We do not love another beyond what is self-interested, or beyond forced blindness to the right, but in fact because of the weakest selfishness which exists on our part—living so that another may provide us the necessary pleasure and justification to live. All relationships, however colored by emotional passion, cannot escape the requirement of exhibiting mutual utility to thrive. Intimacy is a function of repeated interaction and

durable than physical pleasures, whether of body or object, be-cause these are the shallowest and least enduring owing to their dependence upon ephemeral and changing circumstances.

With that said, it is important to recall that as scarcity of any one type of these pleasures increases its value, whenever we assume each type is in equal supply, the above hierarchy holds. Further, this hierarchy suggests that those *tastes* informed by intellect over emotion or physicality (in that order) are supe-rior (*i.e.*, more valuable or utile), because they are developed by an overall superior mechanism. Hence, a patron of the fine arts pursues superior pleasures to that of the petty gambler, not so much because opera is itself intrinsically superior to blackjack (though one can certainly argue that it is), but because it is re-flective of a broadly heightened sense of pleasure—the intellec-tual over physical (whereby gambling is subset to the material realm).

Lastly, just as this hierarchy dictates that a lower pleasure may become more valuable owing to its relative scarcity, this does not imply that one may permissibly trade the entirety of any form of pleasure for another, especially a higher for a low-er. There exists a bounded, absolute threshold which may not be crossed. For example, even if physical pleasure sources are scarcer than intellectual pleasures sources, to completely trade the opportunity of experiencing intellectual pleasure for physi-cal pleasure is impermissible because such would make one functionally identical to animals (absent of agency or intellec-tual depth), which exist inferiorly to us in terms of the richness of pleasures they are able to experience. For this reason, they are apt to humane sacrifice for human pleasure (*e.g.*, for eating) before humans might be for one another, whenever a situation might present itself these dual options. Altogether, the desensi-

---

commonality of understanding and experience, much like a beneficial contract between parent and child or two friends, revoked if exces-sively abusive, thereby nullifying the notion that blood is thicker than utility. Unconditional love, is to live as a surrogate through another. It is to place that self-love for ourselves, but as channeled through an-other, above principle, above freedom, above individual responsibility and constructive achievement. Love must never be taken that far—so as to permit us to lose ourselves and all that we must value above even it—for another. We must be strong enough to realize, that even love, must not master us.

tization which overexposure to one pleasing stimulus may cause (much as with heightened sensitivity to those stimuli to which we are underexposed) encourages both the diversification and rotation of pleasures, so as to keep fresh their vitality and appeal to us. The valuing and pursuit of pleasure is the meeting point of reason and moral imperative.

One of my most enduring discoveries appertaining to being happy is the constant and unremitting exploration of new sources of pleasure and their mastery. From the intellectual to the athletic, from the social to the emotional, neglect not that every sphere of human activity, whatever its origins, may be transformed into a source of human joy. In doing so, boredom is an impossibility, and life a continuous surge of almost overwhelmingly splendid delight. Ambition is the only antidote to boredom, the absence of pain and the desire for pleasure. To want no more is to sign our very death warrant. To seek not, to live not.

The Paradox of Hedonism

Clearly, there permeates in the aforementioned writings a strong flavor of moral hedonism. Though this has been robustly defended, another question arises, as noted by philosophers since time immemorial: can the conscious pursuit of happiness yield happiness? The general consensus is 'no'; this however, is simply incorrect. The reason for this misguided understanding lies in the delineation of a meaningless distinction by ethicists—namely the idea that the happy man is only happy by virtue of pursuing things which make him unconsciously happy; conversely, that whereupon identifying his conscious pursuit of happiness, it would forever elude him. Thus, any moral framework which mandates its actors consciously calculate the happiness to be resultant from their actions as the yardstick of such actions' moral content is doomed, owing to this 'paradox of hedonism' whereby no pleasure will actually result from such premeditated actions, and hence, no moral result shall arise (assuming, as argued here, that what increases pleasure is moral).

This alleged problem arises however only by conceptually conflating the *processes of attaining happiness* with the *experience of happiness* itself. This error is analogous to any form of 'metathought,' most especially involving introspection: in order to analyze oneself, one must consciously think about how one thinks, a process which requires the suspension of normal cognitive activity. One cannot both think and think about his thinking simultaneously; this, however, does *not* mean that thinking is not *always occurring*—it is merely occurring under slightly different circumstances about different things. The same holds true regarding happiness; happiness as an experience is not accessible in the conscious pursuit of it, only because the means which afford it are not of the metacognitive realm, much as they are not pain-inflicting/pleasure-reducing. This is not a revelation: just as the nature of happiness precludes its enjoyment by cutting oneself, so too does it preclude enjoyment through the active thinking about it. There are simply certain phenomenological rules which inherently exist governing the procedures by which it can be experienced, as with all qualitative conditions. This does not mean however, that its active desire prohibits its experience or that its requisite indirect pursuit diminishes its desirability as a qualitative state, but rather that one cannot consciously pursue it *and* experience it simultaneously. This is not problematic, since *one cannot act with such simultaneity toward any goal*—just as with the metathought example.[1]

---

1 This psychological phenomenon, known as the 'Paradox of Simultaneity,' while referring to a wide variety of mental thought processes which follow the ensuing general trend, especially references our ability to analyze the nature of reason (including its constitutive elements, or subtypes) and how its correct application leads to the ideally-qualitative lifestyle, yet our paradoxical inability to simultaneously be both *aware* of its nature (as it is being experientially passed through) and the process by which it ought be applied *and* glean the benefits of the ideally-qualitative existential condition it affords. In short, it may be understood as prohibiting us to 'think about X while simultaneously thinking about thinking about X.' We cannot think two things at once. The same phenomenon applies to the Paradox of Hedonism insofar as pleasure can only be experienced as a byproduct of action, not as an end which may be intentionally pursued in isolation. This is because the former analysis of reason or pleasure is metacognitive and necessarily interferes and/or removes an individual from his normal stream of consciousness (regarding reason) or self-aware action aimed at achieving a particular goal (regarding the pursuit of pleasure). The closest examples of cognitive simultaneity we are afforded exist when one either catches brief and vague 'intuitive glimpses' which reveal the overlap between normative reason (and its subtypes) and our active embodiment of it, or in retrospect when analysis and meta-analysis converge.

Any end which requires means cannot be obtained through the pursuit of the end itself; this is an absurd idea. One must pursue the means which naturally exist before achieving such an end. Analogically, this is like saying that one cannot graduate *summa cum laude* without much hard work; the mere wishing to graduate *summa cum laude* is insufficient; no reasonable person would disagree with this, much as they would not disagree that simply because happiness cannot be pursued directly does not dimin-

---

Summarily, *we may not analyze our thought processes (a metacognitive activity) without disengaging ourselves from them (whereby these thought processes themselves are an example of cognitive activity)*; these two processes are mutually-exclusive and cannot exist simultaneously. As one is cognitive, the other metacognitive, they necessarily interfere with each other, much as two parallel cognitive/metacognitive processes cannot exist simultaneously; our thought-processing channels forbid it. As a corollary to this paradox also stands the Principle of Constitutive Exclusion, meaning that while reason as it exists consists of three components, none of each of those subcomponents can be wholly understood or explanatorily reduced by an appeal to the other two. While they may be explicated or largely understood, they can never be experienced or applied in an adequate manner through the reliance of any one other, or all other, components (and thus nothing short of all three subtypes may yield the overall ideal qualitative state made affordable by reason), and hence, are not fully comprehensible in such a manner (especially as the subtype of *experience* of distinct phenomena is integral in understanding the nature of them). This parenthetical case is evident even with rationality which is only coherent as a concept because it can be consciously rationalized as an activity and the qualitative nature of that experience can be reflected upon, in addition to of course analyzing its distinct consequences, the other aspect of understanding a phenomenon. This two-part rubric for understanding a phenomenon—reflecting upon its nature when experiencing it and subsequently analyzing the results it produces—applies equally to rationality, emotion and experiential learning itself. At the end of the day, living ideally through reason requires continual reflection analytically upon one's nature and one's actions as they are prescribed by reason, yet also a distinct process of commonsensical judgment; while both are necessary, consilience of these two processes can never be adequately had owing to their disparate natures, not to mention the added, complicating fact that these two processes differ not only from one another, but so too do their fundamental natures *between* the three subcomponents of reason. The most we can do is intuit their overlap (the aforementioned 'intuitive glimpses', which admittedly may refer to both processes of a single subtype, or perhaps both processes of two or all three such subtypes) or rationalize it from afar, but never *experience* the results of both processes (for one reason subtype let alone all three) simultaneously, since understanding the nature of each process and its effects would require mutually exclusive and interfering cognitive processes.

ish its value, or the value of those means which secure it and are necessary toward its attainment. Rather, one must consciously identify that pleasure is his end goal (admittedly in isolation and distinct from its actual pursuit), and pursue it through other means which must temporarily assume his full attention. Just because pleasure is a *byproduct* of activities which produce it, does not mean we do not intentionally pursue such activities in order to obtain such pleasure; in fact, we do, and enjoy those activities in the process. Moreover, we *do* intentionally pursue the pleasure derived from such activity *before* undertaking it in premeditation, *after* undertaking it in retrospective appreciative reflection—and most probably intermittently *during* its undertaking as well, consciously and unconsciously. Therefore, the intentional pursuit of pleasure can in fact *coincide* with its experience at times (the 'intuitive glimpses' exception to the more general Paradox of Simultaneity which would generally forbid this simultaneous intention and experience), but more generally occurs before or after its experience. Altogether, these arguments conclusively decapitate objections made on behalf of the Paradox of Hedonism, reemphasize that at least one notable exception (consilience by virtue of 'intuitive glimpses' permitting coincident awareness) exists to the phenomenological limitations regarding the Paradox of Simultaneity and reveal that pleasure even as a byproduct rather than a directly-pursuable end does not vilipend the significance of pleasure if in a form either premeditatedly-sought or retrospectively-valued. Pleasure could validly remain axiologically valued even if only attainable as a byproduct and not through direct pursuit as its own end, as the aforementioned arguments demonstrate.

Essentially, just because happiness cannot often be gleaned through direct conscious pursuit, does not mean that its indirect pursuit is not informed by this conscious desire. This is not a setback for hedonic theories; it is merely the inherent ground rules which exist regulating their being put into actual practice. Hence, any moral theory which prizes pleasure as its ultimate value is not doomed to fail because it recognizes that indirect means must be pursued in order to achieve happiness; this is not a theoretical inconsistency implicating that happiness cannot therefore be the only value we should prize (but rather possibly also the means toward its attainment), but rather an inescapable reality owing to the nature of happiness as an experienceable condition—it is only attainable through indirect means. Because it is the ultimate goal we seek however, it is the ultimate driver of our pursuit of those indirect means which secure it; these indirect means themselves have no value however, other than in their ability to access happiness for us. Without their ability to achieve this end (however indirectly), they are worthless. Thus, pleasure remains the sole plausible moral criterion, even if the specific practice toward its attainment requires indirect means. The fact we cannot simply hook up to a Nozickean Experience Machine is a cruel fate seemingly; our need for autonomy as a prerequisite indirect means toward pleasure seems needlessly effortful and inefficient, since pleasure is the ultimate end we unconditionally and unabashedly seek. Nonetheless, the means by which we must follow toward its pursuit are the domain to be regulated by the rules of morality, and of which shall be later explored.

Moreover, it is important to discredit the idea that pleasures enjoyed, however frequently, become trite, for I know not one who enjoys pain, however novel and fresh. Not once have I encountered a man who, never before electrocuted in his life, would like to be for the sake of new experiences and to ensure he takes not for granted those pleasures to which he is accustomed to experiencing. This is not to argue that certain pleasures can lead to temporary (or, if extremely overexposed, permanent) desensitization and loss of interest (thus encouraging their rotation), but this is certainly not to say that ceaseless pleasurable stimuli are an undesirable fate. Thus, pleasure can certainly be enjoyed and appreciated in isolation from pain, for we need not ever experience the latter to appreciate the former.

The Role of Society in Promoting Pleasure

I have long been consistent in believing that moral behavior is chiefly important because it serves as the criterion for being *worthy* of 'durable' (that is, resistant to degradation) pleasures. In short, moral behavior is the prerequisite to meaningful happiness. Why? The answer is because morality—a topic only lucidly discussed in the context of more than one sentient being[1]—involves a backdrop of social interdependence, or at the very least social interaction. It is not *ad rem* in the life of asocial man in the wilderness, because it refers only to interpersonal relations.[2] 'Social' here refers merely to the necessary co-involvement—whether intellectual, cultural, emotional or physical—of beings required in the optimal flourishing of any one of them. Because we can assert man is a social creature by nature, and achieves fullest self-actualization in the context of societal order, we can already assert that the discipline of ethics is preliminarily applicable in studying his personal habits. More than this however, we can realize that because interpersonal interaction is necessary for realizing the maximal potential of the individual, such interaction affords the capacity for experiencing happiness—a quality certainly present in the entelechy of total potential. If this is the case, and morality broadly articulates the rules by which we are to govern either our temperaments or behaviors (or both) when dealing with others, then morality seems of central concern to the eventual attainment of happiness, which is here defended, in likeminded terms of intellectual, emotional and physical pleasures,[3] as one of only two universal human ends—the other being pain or misery (and similarly possessive of physical, emotional and intellectual forms), the only indisputable harm, and morally evil when intentionally achieved toward an undeserving party.

Thus, morality exists to regulate our behaviors within an interpersonal framework. Because happiness cannot be achieved within a vacuum (and if so, man is, to paraphrase Aristotle, either a god or a beast), since absent the social forum necessary for highest fulfillment, it must be understood as attainable via a set of moral rules.

---

1 'Sentience' here encompasses more than its denotative reference to purely non-intellectual sensation; in this text, it includes all forms of experienceable pleasure—whether intellectual, emotional or bodily.

2 Man-animal relations *do* possess a genuine position in moral philosophy, will be discussed further later, but may be ignored for now.

3 Physical pleasures can be divided into the *corporeal* and the *material*; the former deals with pleasures pertaining directly to bodily sentience, such as an embrace or sex, while the latter entails the enjoyment associated with worldly goods.

Unhappiness

Unhappiness is the antipode of happiness, and thus broadly, the antipode of pleasure. Hence, it is a form of pain. The cause of unhappiness is either external or internal. If it is external, then it exists as either intentional (*e.g.*, immoral behavior directed toward us by the hand of another) or unintentional (*e.g.*, an unfortunate, haphazard event, such as a natural disaster, disease or unforeseen anthropogenic accident). If it is internal, then it is the result of psychological disease, itself intentional or not (*e.g.*, biochemical disorder, self-punishment, guilt, neurosis, etc.). In any of these cases, it is equally disfavored and inherently repulsive. The function of reason is twofold; it is to 1) facilitate the optimal tangible realization of one's productive potential and 2) create the internal psychological factors necessary to permit long-term maximal happiness. Because of this, the appropriate application of reason (as it exists as a tripartite phenomenon) should discourage any non-temporary experience of pain. While pain is inevitable in life, its undue experience and negative effects are not, and can be most effectively minimized through the embodiment of reason. This is because unhappiness (whether internal or external) is the result of an imbalance in at least one of the three components ('subtypes') constituting reason: rationality, emotionality or experiential learning. Pain, a form of sentience as diverse in its incarnations as pleasure, exists in all of these three areas which define the total range of human experience. For example, 'rational' pain might include obsessive-compulsiveness (whereby the afflicted suffers at the hand of intrusive thoughts and seemingly impenetrable logic which mandates pain-inflicting behavior), 'emotional' pain might include a heart-wrenching break-up while 'experiential' pain might include the realization that one's past beliefs fail to prepare one for novel circumstances (*e.g.*, the political revolutionary who realizes that his sworn ideology is flawed or the scientist who bitterly recognizes the falsity of a paradigm he labored under for a lifetime). Duly, all pain is a failure of reason, in one form or another.

If unhappiness is the result of an imbalance in one or more of reason's components (whereby said imbalance constitutes either a deficiency or excess within said subpart of reason), then conversely, happiness must result from the harmonious and sustainable balancing of reason's subparts with each other. To this end, unhappiness must be understood as the result of unreason, and hence, the result of immoral behavior, for the two are coincident. Such immoral behavior is either the result of undeserved self-harm (immoral intrapersonal action) or pain created from knowledge of lacked desert of happiness, the result of injurious behaviors toward others (immoral interpersonal action). Equally, what is extreme is always immoral. Immoral behavior must result in pain because in cases of interpersonal harm, we recognize morality to be a social phenomenon reliant upon others since fundamentally concerned with issues of equitable relations between parties. Hence, knowledge of violation of such contractual equity cannot result except in simultaneous knowledge of unworthiness to profit from it, or until our wrongs are rectified. A hermit may indeed concern himself only with intrapersonal benefit (though never ignorant that moral behavior spreads pleasure, itself a good, and hence cause for contenting knowledge), but his is a bankrupt morality incapable of attaining the highest pleasures of intellectual and emotional stimulation, present only in the socializing processes of the exchange of ideas and love and friendship. Even the loner may understand the intrinsic good affordable by sympathetic reasoning, even if absent palpable self-interest—that recognition that we are all equivalent agents in terms of our hedonic nature and inclination to satisfy it—and hence unexcused from claiming ignorance regarding moral ideality, as opposed to mere acceptability.

Moral behavior concerns itself as much with those hedonic actions concerning only our own welfare as much as that of others, and for this reason, is inextricably linked to our own happiness. Since the allocation of pleasure is a necessarily moral act, and as pleasure is the only moral good and its concern a necessarily ethical issue, to behave morally requires that we both provide pleasure unto ourselves, and are worthy of pleasure through equitable actions that we perform toward others, receiving utile compensation in return for such labors. In justice toward external parties, we deserve self-directed pleasures, since the latter are ultimately borne by the labors of others, toward whom without due recompense paid on our part robs us of joys otherwise the result of exploitation and hence, no longer subject to enjoyment. For, a piacular pleasure, that is, one ill-gotten, is not one to be enjoyed at all.

While reason cannot provide an impervious defense against the experience of *all* unhappiness (for such is the inefficiency of the human will when pitted against a world far-more resolute in its determination to infect its inhabitants with cruelty), it can, in the hands of the strong-willed, provide for one against all long-term or intense displeasure. This is because the experience of pain prompts one to recognize the imbalance(s) responsible for its existence, while conscious discipline permits one to rectify said imbalance via the appropriate measures (*e.g.*, the heartbroken Ivy League reject must recognize his unhappiness the result of excessive emotionality which must be countered by heightened rationality prompting him to realize that one's university bodes only negligibly in a successful future). Often, the imbalance in one reason subtype is balanced by adjusting the levels of others (as opposed to working in isolation to adjust the level of the imbalanced subtype in question—while this latter option is admittedly viable, it requires a greater degree of discipline since this is a troubled area to begin with, unlike others, which can be otherwise adjusted with lesser adversity and resistance to change, for pain proves a most stubborn intruder reluctant to be tampered with or eradicated).

External negative (pain-causing) circumstances can understandably promote misery. However, such sorrow should desist upon recognizing that one has acted to his fullest reasonable capacity to prevent such unfortunate events before their occurrence, and to eliminate them once first encountered; if unsuccessful, solace may be had for they were beyond one's reasonable control to avoid and hence only now, should be accepted. The alternative is to receive them with continued despair—a self-evidently inferior alternative, in hedonic terms. Critics will be quick to point out that certain circumstances exist which are so overwhelmingly negative that no one could learn to endure them stolidly; if this is ever truly the case, for few circumstances exist in actuality of such intense and enduring quality, then because the only value of life exists in its pleasurable experience, suicide or euthanasia may become a morally- and rationally-preferable action. To kill under these circumstances is not wrong because no act is intrinsically wrong, but only so if it deprives one of a life of future pleasure. For, a life without that promise is worthless. Such legitimate recourse however, for reasons owing to potential abuse, should always be held with the greatest suspicion and reluctance. Rather, it is both morally- and rationally-advisable to combat such unhappiness with an adjustment in reason sub-types. In doing so, one may prohibit long-term or disproportionate periods of grief (as well as pleasure, which, when existent in extreme bursts, can too prove ultimately destabilizing of long-term optimality and reason) through the conscious engineering of harmonious levels of each of reason's three components. The same holds even truer in cases of internal unhappiness, for such stems from self-directed causes, and can thus be eradicated more efficiently since both the cause of despair *and* its received effects are both wholly within one's control (unlike with external causes, whereupon we possess control only over our response to them). This of course assumes that we possess fundamental control in altering or responding to the internal causes of our pleasure or displeasure in question (*e.g.,* redeeming the guilt from a knowingly wrongful act), as opposed to succumbing to forces beyond such control, for example mental illness.

Justifying Moral Practice

Being moral when it is difficult to do so ultimately comes down to a matter of our selfish preoccupation with desert. Because we cannot escape recognition that moral behavior achieves maximization of the good—of pleasure—and that such behavior both entitles us to due reciprocity on the part of others and to pleasure reveling in our knowing we achieved the good, our ultimate impetus to behave justly stems from its permitting us happiness, either directly through the mutual benefitting of one another, or singularly, whereby knowledge of desert is both a prerequisite to further non-desert-related pleasures of which we pursue, and itself pleasing in that we acknowledge our own goodness. He who finds behaving morally inconvenient has a mind not properly attuned to his priorities, for none is so central as the safety of our happiness. To illegitimately obtain it is to not be able to experience it at all; immoral behavior taints its short-term happiness with a guilt far costlier than the initial courage required to do what was not easy, but right. And, whereas guilt is found only among possessors of conscience, this must predictably convince us to behave otherwise. Pursuit of the good is more than cleansing of our conscience, but appeals to the objective righteousness of universal fairness rather than biased self-interest, to that sense of decorum regarding the manner in which we should live in order to be worthy of its highest glory, happiness. We may not ever be able to shake off the inevitable truth of desert without becoming barbarians; such is the guarantor of our unique humanity. Being moral, best evidenced when in fact it is difficult, ensures us of our commitment to our convictions, providing edifying pleasures even beyond those which do not require hardship. For, the greatest joys are born from the greatest sufferings, but nonetheless resilient in the wake of our highest sense of what it means to lead a worthwhile life—to live according to those principles which make us worthy of happiness. I am not saying that there are not temporarily sated immoral men, but I am saying that the thinking man attainable of the highest joys of life through just conduct and knowledge of his moral desert of happiness cannot lead this type of lifestyle. He cannot live in both worlds and extract their opposing benefits. One who realizes morality is real and important cannot be happy knowing he is not worthy of benefit which comes about at someone else's expense; the guilt is crushing. Choosing the values one will prioritize in life is a matter of proclaiming the type of happiness we crave. The knowingly immoral can never achieve true happiness, for they are certain to realize they possess what is undeservingly theirs. Such knowledge can always attempt to be suppressed beneath the consciousness, but never successfully, for the edicts of reason shall invariably percolate to the surface of our self-awareness. Morality is more important than life, for without the former, no deserved joy could exist in the latter. And, a joy undeserved is one not at all, instead a blunt torture acknowledging our unworthiness, for no happiness may thrive unless its possessor is confident of his moral desert of it. As for myself, I rather deserve to die than be unworthy to live.

Summary

So, why be moral? If the answer is not yet obvious, perhaps the following summation shall cast away any lingering obscurities and bring forth our solution with stinging clarity. Pleasure, quite simply, is the only undisputed good. This is important because, as I see it, the whole nature of axiology is one which must be understood as identifying the link between an inherently valued end and the proper and most efficient actions which obtain it via an examination of the nature of said good. Hence, we recognize ethics as a subset of axiology insofar as pleasure is the pursued end we value, moral rules the legitimate means by which we deserve and/or become entitled to its experience and possession. Such rules ensure that the very value of the good pursued is not opposed or outweighed by means which contradict it or reverse its effects. Moreover, they divulge the method by which the good should be pursued, and must always be the product of reason. I assume here that morality itself is valuable because it achieves some conception of the good, and because that good—pleasure—is inherently valuable, and as its own end, it ought to be the stuff of a worthwhile life. This good supersedes each of our subjective interests, and valuable for this very reason—that it is larger than each of us. That is why, to put it another way, ethics *is* what we do when no one else is looking. Answering 'how ought we live?' is the most important question of all, for its solution singularly permits us to find happiness, the only indisputable good. Ethics, of which branch of knowledge this question squarely falls within, therefore becomes the most important subject. Whereas ethics deals with identifying proper person-to-person behavior, politics is but a mere extension of ethics from this interpersonal perspective to a macroscopic one which seeks maximizing the good, and something to be later elaborated.

Specifically, and ultimately, whatever maximizes the good is the greatest moral good. This principle, the *Value Maximizing Imperative (VMI)*, is the result of elementary logic; if X is valued, maximizing its experience within and among individuals is preferable to its non-maximal experience, whereby maximization is dependent upon situational constraints. Because morality is simply the framework to achieve an axiological end or value, whatever is most axiologically prized is also the most moral value to pursue. Obtaining the highest value must always be prioritized as the highest objective for moral action. Thus, VMI relates not only to the general moral imperative to quantitatively maximize experience of the good, but the moral imperative to first prioritize the quantitative maximization of the highest *qualitative* good. Further, it requires us to treat agent preferences equally unless considerations of individual merit, utility output and desert become circumstantially relevant, so as to cloak ourselves behind a Rawlsian veil of ignorance necessary for impartial treatment within a framework of utility-producing resource distribution. The most valued good(s) achieved to the furthest extent possible is often subject to the situation determining the highest value to prize, and thus moral thinking requires a great flexibility of thought made possible by reason. Such statements however, do *not* necessarily advocate a utilitarian approach without further analysis. The philosophical reality of our situation proves far more complex than to furnish so hasty a conclusion, as is to be shown.

PART IV: WHAT IS MORAL

IN THIS SECTION, we shall transition from a broad over-view of hedonism as the foremost moral theory toward a more comprehensive explication of its tenets. Namely, this shall entail a rigorous exploration of what is normatively prescribed by a he-donic axiology, against a backdrop of moral naturalism, which argues that what is moral follows directly from the natural con-dition of a being and its capacities. For animals, this includes only force[1]; for humans, only reason. Morality cannot exist but when one is faithful to the noblest incarnation of his nature. Be-cause morality, of any stripe, is sensible only if coincident with the nature of its practitioner, and man universally possesses the appropriate nobility in his blood, the 'is' of his being commands the 'ought' of his moral obligation. And, as in the case of human morality where there is one rule with countless exceptions, let us divine both the law and its exemptions.

---

1 Beyond unnecessary displeasure or inhumane treatment, animals do not possess equal moral considerations as men because they lack those essential capacities for pleasure which demand careful treatment—the intellect, followed by emotion, possessing, only in part, the most primi-tive manifestations of physical joys. Because they cannot aspire to the same heights of pleasure, they are not our moral equals, hence revealing the forceful reality that a hierarchy of pleasure exists.

Utilitarian Reasoning

Morality must be functionalist; all moral theories and directives ought have a tangible purpose which is ultimately promoting of utility. Moral goods cannot transcend sentient experience, the extent of our capacity for comprehension, and thus, only the utile is relevant. Thus, those superstitions, traditions, object worship and blind loyalties—whether institutional or spiritual—which retard utility ought to be abolished. This book is ultimately a stalwart defense of utilitarianism, albeit one with significant modifications and a renewed interpretation regarding the merit of disparate theories. Hedonism, as is known, holds that the production of pleasure is the criterion in determining whether an action is moral; if an act promotes the former, it is moral, and if contrary to this end, it is immoral. (For now, we can disregard the role of intent in discussions of the morality of an action.) It is intuitive to see how this position can lead to utilitarianism, for whatever maximizes pleasure amongst persons (the goal of utilitarianism) clearly reflects the hedonic attitude that pleasure is the only good. According to the VMI, whatever maximizes this good is undoubtedly preferable to less-maximizing alternatives. Intuitive as this may appear, the link between simple hedonism and utilitarianism—especially the brand to be advocated here—requires sturdier support.

A central feature to morality is its objectivity. No moral philosophy which indefensibly advocates the interests of certain parties over others can prove reasonable or valid; rather, what is moral in situation A must not only be so in situations B through Z, but apply per unchanging terms for all rational agents. To change the standards for moral action between situations or individuals is to invalidate the fundamental idea behind all of ethics: that what is ethical is so because of something *intrinsic* to a particular form of behavior, something which produces an indisputable good—in this case, pleasure in all its forms. It is this very unchangeability of moral sentiments which gives them their value. If one discounts this view, then the entirety of ethics becomes a kaleidoscope of whim. Not only is this intuitively the wrong approach, but demonstrably so considering an alternative framework of complete consistency in its moral treatment of all situations and agents is in fact viable.

Utilitarianism is the only consequentialist moral theory which is agent-neutral. This means two things: first, that deon-tological theories have the capacity for agent-neutrality (that is, they equally prioritize the moral preferences of agents, including the actor himself, pursuing interests exclusive to one another), and that all other consequentialist frameworks do not, including ethical egoism and altruism. Egoism unjustifiably places the de-mands of the actor himself above the interests of others, whereas altruism unjustifiably prioritizes the demands of others—col-lectively or individually—above the actor. While collective in-terest often may prove more morally pressing than individual concern, the reason behind this must be further explored before actually defended. For now, we may conclude that both egoism and altruism are agent-subjective, indefensibly valuing the in-terests of one individual or group over another. Because morality must be objective in recognizing the moral equality of differing perspectives and their interests, we find that only utilitarianism passes this test as a consequentialist theory. Additionally, utili-tarianism ultimately possesses an aura of natural intuitiveness; that is, it is reflective of the macroscopic concerns of forces and biological processes beyond our control. If the barest purpose of life is the promulgation of genetic material, then survival of the greatest number of the most utile becomes the order of the day. Much as we may wish to believe otherwise, God is an utilitarian.

But, what about deontology? Why should deontological theories not hold a place on the mantle of moral consideration, whether agent-neutral or not? The reason lies in the distinction between what each school of thought prizes; consequentialists argue the moral worth of an act lies in its tangible consequences, deontologists its intent as pertains to obedience to an immutable moral rule. Why therefore, should consequences trump inten-tions? Surely one soon realizes the dangers of an ethics grounded only in outcomes and absent of any absolute proscriptions. For, in a discussion in which all options are on the table, however horrid, the mere placing them under consideration heightens the likelihood of their enactment. In theory, seeking obedience to a universal moral law with maximal reasonable efficiency decreas-es the probability of this fear being realized; in practice 'utile rules' with exceptionality clauses (meaning rule utilitarianism) generally forbid those egregious acts considered possible under a non-deontological framework.

Lexical Priorities and Hedonic Transfer

A common strand of thought in utilitarian theories is the idea that special, bounded limitations should be placed on actions which are the result of forced choice between unequal utility-producing alternatives. The rationale behind this nuance is an attempt to preempt objections regarding the brutish lengths to which one may permissibly go in order to maximize happiness (say, killing 1,000 people to save 1,001). To be precise, we may operationally define *lexical priorities as the identification of those limits which forbid the trading-off of one axiological value for another, regardless of the quantity of either.* For example, utilitarians will argue for the maximization of happiness, but, assuming they consider preserving life the highest good (since it is the prerequisite to all further hedonic experience), it is likely they shall argue that even one life ought never be sacrificed even if necessary in the name of achieving a lesser good, such as rescuing all the art in the Louvre from destruction. For lexical prioritists, life is a nontradable entity. 100 units of random value X can never be substituted for 1 unit of life. This is a logic I believe to be careless, cowardly and naïve.

Whereas lexical priorities might appear intuitive at first, upon closer examination they fail the test of reason for two reasons. Firstly, they fail to appreciate that the only legitimate moral groundwork is a hedonic axiology—that is, all moral actions must ultimately be so defined by their capacity for rendering pleasure. Secondly, they misrecognize the implications of the agent-neutrality of utilitarianism. While Rawls correctly noted that pleasure is non-aggregable within the individual (that is, two happy individuals are not morally preferable if it meant sacrificing the happiness of one individual since the furthest extent of experience falls within each individual's consciousness, separate and unfungible), he failed to recognize the preferability of utility-maximization at the expense of individuals *from a third-person point-of-view.* Herein lies one of the great divergences between consequentialism and deontology, and the importance of clarity in reconciling these two schools from this first bifurcation cannot be overstated.

Hedonic transfer refers to the moral preferability of maximizing utility without regard for lexical priorities by recognizing utility as a functionally aggregable entity. Note in this definition that utility is understood only as 'functionally aggregable'—that is, while we recognize the separation of consciousness which prohibits pleasure from being experienced or sensibly understood beyond the realm of one individual, such does not prevent its being morally preferred from an objective, third-party viewpoint. We understand that if Agent X were sacrificed to save five others, none of the five would either a) benefit more personally than Agent X if he were spared (and the five others perished) or b) possess an 'accumulative collective happiness' which would outweigh the happiness experienced in his one life, because happiness cannot be aggregated across separate consciousnesses. We fully understand this point, but disagree that X should not be sacrificed. Permit one deviation, however.

Intuition is perhaps the sharpest double-edged sword known to man. On the one hand, without it, we would be absent of the good judgment necessary in quotidian decisions, resulting in our perpetually-effortful consternation and conscious deliberation. Such ceaseless contemplation would quickly turn to intense mental strain, the pain of which would soon become unbearable, rendering us paralyzed. Contrarily however, intuition provides us with a heuristic which is not always suitable to circumstance. For example, is it intuitive that a table is comprised of mostly empty space? Atomic physics tell us such is so. Or that the Earth is not flat, after all? To this day I still wrestle fathoming otherwise. Prior to the idea of separation of consciousness, for most, the utilitarian position wins *de facto*; it is intuitive. It is equally instinctive and advisable to support the proposition that a society ought not allow itself to perish before sacrificing the few toward conscription, that progressive taxation ought to redistribute wealth to the greatest possible number, much as classroom instruction should cater for the lowest common denominator. The greatest good—that is, the greatest number capable of receiving positive effectuation—is a virtually axiomatic moral principle, confirmed in its objectivity as much for its visibly absent appeal to selfish interests. However, upon realizing that experience—toothsome or not—cannot sensibly extend beyond the individual, prompts one to undergo a dramatic intellectual reversal, the results of which lead to certain staggering and unacceptable outcomes. The outcomes, of course, are not unacceptable by virtue of their implications, however, so much as they are a deficiency of properly-applied reason.

Morality must be an objective enterprise. This means that its interests must align themselves with those which exist beyond selfish concerns, though the two, for reasons other than the nature of the latter, can coincide as a result of happenchance. It is understandable that a man's first instinctive priority is the self-love he hath for himself, and those which fuel his most immediate happiness. This is a natural fact we cannot resist; it is as inherent as our genetic code. Nonetheless, moral science is an intellectual discipline not dependent upon whim or vested profit, but the application of reason both normative and pursuant to empirical investigations. Whereas one man cannot care more for others than himself without contrived artifice, the duty of morality as an extrapersonal arbiter, as one whose concerns far transcend those of the individual, typifies its relationship to something greater than us all—something pure, complete and independent of itself: the truth as fruit of reason. Accordingly, agent-neutrality is a central ingredient to all moral formulations; separate consciousnesses are defeated as a legitimate obstacle to utilitarian ethics *because they cannot sustain agent-neutrality*. This is because deontological respect for the individual (what follows from respecting separate consciousnesses), holds only so long as there does not exist a forced choice in which either alternative prevents this respect. In this case, deontology fails us, and provides us no acceptable alternative. The immediate objection to this claim as raised by deontologists will cite the moral permissibility of omission in certain situations; this argument shall be flattened in a following section.

Before continuing, we must further refine what has thus far been said. Lexical priorities which exist not as utile rules (a plausible idea to be later discussed), but as inherent pieces of moral machinery, do so only as a result of misguidedness. The reason being that all moral propositions must ultimately collapse into a hedonic axiology, for reasons already articulated. Thus, any value other than pleasure which is prioritized above it becomes invalid, as does the lexical prioritization behind it. What does this leave us? In the sudden absence of lexical priorities, we find only pleasure and its maximization our compelling duty. But, are there certain limitations upon this mandate? Does this rule confine itself only to sentient beings? Loyalty and autonomy may not be above pleasure (let alone of any value except in the procreation of the latter), but since these qualities are only comprehensible to sentient beings, does this imply we are morally confined to their concern? The answer is usually, though not exclusively. Hedonic transfer, as previously mentioned, refers to the permissible aggregation of pleasure. Judging moral action from a neutral third-party vantage point permits us to understand hedonism as a top-down approach, unlike the bottom-up, individual-outward approach of deontology. This means that, like VMI informs us, maximization of the good (which in this case, and every other, is pleasure) requires an analysis of the likely endstates of actors in a situation; that is, how much happiness will how many experience. Because this notion preserves the objectivity of a moral actor not pliant to the particular interests of one over another for unjustifiable reasons (though justifiable ones exist, as will be later shown, we shall temporarily ignore them), the moral actor can maintain his dispassion and act appropriately. In a situation of forced choice, in which deontological principles are unsustainable (*e.g.,* the trolley problem, in which the actor must participate in the killing of at least one individual—a deontologically forbidden act), hedonic transfer not only provides us with a way out, but with a superior justification; it recognizes that while pleasure is not sensible beyond the individual *personally,* it is so *rationally.* This is critical, for the former requires us to think of the killing of one as qualitatively identical to the killing of all (for one cannot experience beyond himself), while the latter recognizes that from a third-party viewpoint, the endstates of the greatest number matter more, because the good is experienced by more persons. Basically, hedonic transfer allows us to judge the happiness of individuals as the furthest extent of its reach, but that maximizing the number capable of its experience is superior to a lesser number experiencing it because though not extrapersonally experience-able, we can understand from a third-party viewpoint that such maximization is still preferable as that good is experienceable *on an individual level*, more so than it otherwise might be. The happi-ness delivered constitutes the entire phenomenological world of someone, and the creation of such a pleasing world, even if inca-pable of being experientially shared, can still be empathetically and rationally understood as the good. This unique approach to logic is a central pillar supporting utilitarianism, and one which shall prove this school the better of all others.

Hedonic transfer presents us with an understanding of life as an empty vessel, whose only worthwhile purpose is the ex-perience of pleasure. In this regard, a life can be quantitatively understood as capable of holding, say, 100 hedons—or units of pleasure—at any given time. Assuming one possesses control over the distribution of utility-producing resources, these units are to be transferred so long as they are experienced with greater intensity by one or fewer other(s), or, less intensely but more diffusely amongst a greater number of others. Hedonic transfer views pleasure as a fluid commodity, to be distributed with such classically utilitarian purpose as this, and morally permissible because its oversight is achieved through use of a third-party ar-biter monitoring the transfer of such utility-producing resources. This eliminates the issue of separation of consciousness, insofar as it recognizes maximizing the number of individuals' pleasure is superior to a lesser number, even if pleasure cannot be expe-rienced beyond the individual, because a top-down/omniscient perspective informs us the prior scenario permits the greatest good to be experienced *even within the limitations of individual experi-ence*. Essentially, even if happiness is only experienceable to the individual, maximizing the number of experiential domains in which it may be received is still preferable to a reduced number. It is analogous to soldiers being equipped for battle from the im-partial stance of the general; while a rifle may only be of use to a single soldier (it cannot be operated by more than one person at a time), maximizing the number of rifles distributed to the greatest number of soldiers is preferable relative to distributing fewer rifles. The latter scenario spells disaster in battle, while the former heightens the prospects of victory, the ultimate goal. For deontologists who find the notion that individuals may be used as means to an end abhorrent, it is more logical to prevent the good from being experienced by the greatest number to the greatest extent possible for each (as through experiences which fill their individual consciousnesses), if at the cost of altering the *status quo* whereby the good may be experienced by fewer. This is the antithesis of impartiality, *for it unjustifiably prioritizes the pleasure of some* (often the few) *over the pleasure of others* (often the greater), and is analogous to a general preferring to permit one soldier ten rifles (only one of which he may use) because he found an added nine in a barren field, rather than distributing the remainder to nine additional unarmed servicemen.

Object transfer is an idea subset to hedonic transfer, and extends the latter principle to objects (or more broadly, all utility-producing insentient entities), as well as persons. If we can understand the value of life as a broadly quantifiable entity—existing along a hedonic continuum[1]—then every life has the capacity for experiencing a finite quantity and intensity of *hedons*, or pleasurable moments (*dolors* being the converse term for displeasurable moments). If this is the case, then not only ought we recognize the moral value of trading lives (if forced choice requires) insofar as its capacity for hedonic maximization by virtue of hedonic transfer, but so too must we recognize the hedonic impact of inanimate objects upon such lives, for the latter can certainly add hedons to living persons, and thus must not be neglected from calculation. A clear example of the importance

---

1 A hedonic continuum lends a comparatively objective approach in the moral evaluation of lives. Assuming that pleasure is roughly quantifiable (insofar as certain pleasures are uncontroversially superior to others in quality and/or intensity when looked at relative to one another, if not in isolation), we may propose a scale as follows: $-100 \leq x < 0$ hedonic units constitute all that which is displeasing, in increasing intensity toward -100, and may be termed *dolors*; 0 represents hedonic neutrality (that is, neither pleasure nor pain), while $0 < x \leq +100$ represents pleasure, in increasing intensity toward +100, termed *hedons*. Intensity, duration, quality and 'purity' (or pleasure/pain achieved without accompanying contrary painful/pleasurable sensation) are four qualities which partially contribute to the assessment of a hedonic numeration. Absolute numerical precision is not our goal or wholly achievable, but rather that generalized quantification of competing pleasures for purposes of assessment and relative prioritization is possible.

of this principle at work is the following: imagine only one of the following groups can be saved: (Group 1) 2 persons, each of whose lives average 90 hedons; or (Group 2) 5 persons, each of whose lives average 20 hedons. (For the sake of simplicity, let us presently assume their life expectancy, likelihood of changes in hedonic numeration [or, the amount of pleasure experienced/quality of life], etc. identical—factors which, if variant, could greatly complicate calculations.) According to the principle of hedonic transfer, it is not only morally preferable but morally binding that the first group ought to be saved. Why?

The answer is in the math:

$$2 \times +90 = 180 \text{ hedons (Group 1)}$$
$$5 \times +20 = 100 \text{ hedons (Group 2)}$$

Let us turn to what an instance of object transfer might look like. Imagine two groups, only one of which can be saved: (Group 1) 50 persons, each with an average of 60 hedons, or (Group 2) a young Thomas Edison. Assuming the latter's life carried on in this thought experiment exactly as it did in reality (and that we could foresee as such), the solution to our problem becomes obvious: whereas the first group possesses a significant hedonic numerated value: 50×60 hedons = 3000 hedons, the hedonic value of Thomas Edison is intuitively far greater. Understanding why leads us to some important realizations. First, it matters little how happy Edison himself may have been in life, for even if he lived a life of whose every moment possessed 100 hedon-value, this would pale in comparison to Group 1—3000 hedons (assuming an average of 60 per person per moment) versus his paltry 100. Second, it immediately illustrates the importance of *utility output* as a vital ingredient in moral calculations and thus lends itself as an example of object transfer. Edison is ultimately responsible for the generation of more utility, more hedons, than Group 1, because of his inert inventions: the motion picture, the phonograph, the electric light bulb. These are *objects* which themselves have produced virtually immeasurable pleasure for billions of individuals for over a century. Thus, objects can have significant impact on the pleasure experienced, and may carry greater moral weight than even the lives of particular individuals, if their experience may be visited upon a far greater number in sufficient intensity. An obvious example (made so by virtue of its extremeness) of this principle might arise if preserving the contents of the Museo del Prado required the sacrifice of a handful of relatively low-utile or negatively-utile (that is, those who produce net pain rather than pleasure) agents. Clearly, the enduring cultural and hedonic significance of such a vast collection of priceless artifacts for millions would outweigh the potential utility of even some human beings. By recognizing that there are no inviolable boundaries between the trading of lives (nor the the trading of lives for inanimate objects) in both the doctrines of hedonic and object transfer, leads us to abolishing the moral legitimacy of lexical priority altogether. It is important to affirm that object transfer carries with it moral considerations only so long as objects may reasonably be predicted to affect the lives of others, even if indirectly; where such effectuation is not anticipated however, objects are to carry no moral bearing, for their value is only in the pleasurable consumption by sentient beings.

The intellectual underpinnings of object transfer advocate that objects, and by extension, knowledge and actions, have no innate 'moral aura,' but rather may be converted toward moral— or for that matter, immoral—purposes. No information or object exists possessive of a haloed nature, and hence may be, whatever its origin, directed toward a moral or immoral purpose by means of our intended actions. While certain of the scientists behind the advent of modern rocketry may have been Nazis, to disregard the undeniable utility of their findings would be reckless since their discoveries were themselves amoral, and, while perhaps initially commissioned for purposes of evil, could undoubtedly be redirected toward purposes of good—from modern satellite installations to space exploration. From good may be born evil, and from evil good. The question is not one of innateness ascribed to these qualities, but the individual choices of conscience when confronted with them. Dovetailed with the idea of morality being a matter of choice and not inherence is the rejection of all symbolism and tradition which is utility-decreasing. While these activities may hold utility insofar as they are emotionally gratifying and uniting amongst people (*e.g.*, the British adoration of monarchy as a unique cultural source of common identity), they are just as often divisive, destructive and irrational—from religious extremism and discrimination to the more innocuous yet utile-minimizing sexual mores which discourage premarital sex, the latter of which misguidedly elevate its moral status beyond that of a principally physical, but rather partly spiritual, act.

Meritocratic Utilitarianism: An Overview

All students of philosophy may reflexively recite the mantra of classical utilitarianism (CU): 'what is moral is that which achieves the greatest happiness for the greatest number.' Very clearly, the Greatest Happiness Principle is grounded upon the *numerical* maximization of pleasure. Of course, utilitarians since then have nuanced the debate regarding a hierarchy of pleasures, act versus rule utility, an agent's motives, etc. Nevertheless, at the heart of all utilitarian theories is the idea that happiness ought be experientially maximized, and that in order to do this, utility-producing or utile resources must be distributed in such a way so as to maximize the minimal amount ('maximinize') of happiness experienceable by any subset number of persons within the total set of individuals relevant to a given situation. Thus, ensuring a minimal, universal hedonic standard for all members of a class takes priority over exhausting utility-producing resources to maximize the happiness of a first individual before diverting them toward increasing the happiness of any second or subsequent individual. An example: imagine there are 10 survivors stranded in the desert following an unfortunate plane crash, and each is desperately thirsty. There is enough water to either sustain the survival of all 10, though satisfying none of their thirst, or sufficient water to fully satisfy the thirst of one at the expense of not sustaining 9 others. Clearly, the former is the moral course of action. Thus, most utilitarians are not simply interested in maximizing the *mean* happiness experienceable by a given individual or set of individuals (for that fails to ensure maximization of such happiness's distribution among the widest possible number, as 1 individual averaging 64 hedons and 9 others averaging 4 hedons are otherwise morally equivalent to 10 individuals each with 10 hedons), but in maximizing the lowest common quantity of happiness experienceable by each member of the set of individuals affected.[1]

Meritocratic utilitarianism (MU) offers a more defensible alternative compatible with the features of other moral theories relative to the versions of maximin utilitarianism described above. In short, it stands as the cornerstone and most perfected understanding of my view of what constitutes moral behavior, and exists as the starting point for ethical action in all spheres of human endeavor, ranging from politics to aesthetics. In short, it is the very cornerstone of the grand unified theory of ethics herein presented.

MU is, like all utilitarian theories, a derivation of hedonism, arguing that pleasure is the only moral value, and that sensibly, its maximization is ideal. However, while it mandates the maximization of pleasure, it does not so *quantitatively*—that is, the maximization of the intensity, duration, quality and purity of pleasure to the greatest number, whether calculated totally (maximizing the added total of the happiness of individuals within a group together) or averagely (maximizing the average total of happiness as experienced by each individual within a group)—but rather *meritocratically*, or according to each individual's utility output. This is the first critical difference between MU and all other utilitarian theories: utility is not to be distributed without reason, but in direct proportion to the utility produced by individual agents within a given *contextual frame* (CF). *A contextual frame refers to any set of parameters which define the scope of an action's utile impact or estimated potential impact; these include chronological, geographic, probabilistic and magnitude-based (number of individuals affected, and to what degree or intensity) factors.* As a general rule, calculations of potential utile output should prioritize the present, followed by the future and lastly the past, in order of experiential importance. As the past has already occurred, nothing may alter it. The present is what is currently traveled through, and the future never guaranteed, but ever-becoming our present.

---

1 There is significant debate as to whether this lowest common hedonic denominator ought be achieved if it involves the distribution of utility-producing resources so thinly amongst a wide number of persons that the benefit each receives is negligible, versus a smaller number affected but non-negligibly. We shall resume and conclude this debate later.

Only the present is an experiential reality. Assuming pleasures of the future and present are equal, always pursue and prioritize them in the present. Once in the past, we are permitted the small boon of reliving them as memories. Thus, while concerns of equity must always trace themselves into past actions, and hence are critical, when such demands cannot be met, the present and future must take priority, the future only trumping the present if more is likely to be held at stake than as opposed to contemporarily. More will be discussed regarding contextual frames later.

Why ought pleasure not be distributed willy-nilly? It is axiomatic that pleasure is its own good, and it has already been demonstrated that it is the only such intrinsic good known to humans. Accordingly, it would be perfectly sensible that its maximization is moral, regardless of the utility output of individuals. However, we live in a world of limited supply, and limitless demand. *Pleasure, in every sense, is the result of resource allocation and expenditure.* Virtually no pleasure may be derived freely, or without effort. Its formation requires the use, consumption and/or distribution of utility-providing resources, of whose usage often ensures the application of pleasure-reducing (or pain-increasing) effort, thus limiting the availability of 'free pleasures'— those pleasures which are produced by pleasurable activity itself (*e.g.*, sexual intercourse, whereby each actor contributes to the happiness of the other whilst simultaneously gaining pleasure himself/herself). Because the production of pleasure thus requires the use and distribution of resources, ranging from material goods to physical action (itself the result of caloric intake) or effortful mental thought (as in the writing of this philosophical treatise, hoped to bring eventual happiness to many readers), which themselves are necessarily scarce, the total possible production of pleasure it itself finite. An infinite supply of pleasure cannot be generated, because only finite pleasure-producing or pleasure-enabling resources exist, including the organic molecules which compose our very mortal person. (Of course, if such an infinite supply of utile resources existed, classical utilitarian reasoning advocating unqualified hedonic quantitative maximization would make sense for all non-negative utility providers, for to provide for the harmful would constitute an injustice, as to be later explained.)

Because of the scarcity of utile resources, their distribution must be most judiciously handled, hence the necessity of merit-based resource distribution in my conception of MU. It is understood that while the maximization of pleasure is preferable (hence the utilitarian aspect to the theory), there exist implementation constraints to that maximization insofar as the finite supply of resources which provide such pleasure (hence the meritocratic aspect as well). This may appear reasonable enough, but a soon-menacing question rears its beastly head: *how* are we to measure merit? No doubt, the very notion of merit-based utility distribution forebodes a sinister world of self-justifying elitist rule and a sophistical defense of massive inequality amongst persons. Quite simply, this philosophy makes no pretensions to be anything other than an impassioned apology for elitism—the mere belief that certain individuals are superior to others. Little else is more obvious a fact in both nature and society than the hierarchy which exists among persons, whether it be framed in terms of intellect, morality, beauty or personal industry. People are *not* created equal, and before this reality shall be perverted into the engineered indignation of mass opposition and the following qualifications omitted, let them be averred with the greatest emphasis. Simply, this natural and moral hierarchy of men is reflective of their disparate contributions to the welfare of our race.

There is nothing particularly fair about nature. It is neither just nor cruel, though the consequences of its reality are seldom a source of indifference for its inhabitants. Nature is amoral, and cares not for our grumblings and outrages at its perceived injustices and brutality. It cares not at the fear of young zebras who watch as their mother is ripped apart by a pack of ravenous hyenas, much as it does nothing to prevent certain mothers afflicted with AIDS from transmitting the disease to their newborns, effectively rendering a death sentence upon those not yet given the opportunity to live. The injustices of mental retardation, natural catastrophes and inherited defects may all be extreme instances of nature's indifference to our—and others'— cause, but it speaks to the important fact that equality, fairness and justice are not elements guaranteed to us in this world, and certainly not so by the provisions of nature. Such inequity is not confined to the natural realm either, for despite its greater malleability, societal circumstances are only mildly pliable; just as infeasible as it would be to establish total equalization of social goods and resources from $t0$, such a feat would immediately become undone in the unregulated interactions of economic exchange between parties, rapidly creating large inequalities of wealth—the result of variances in personal industry, itself the result of natural endowments, luck, disparities in business experience, self-honed merit, etc. (A defense of *why* such interactions ought remain fundamentally unregulated nevertheless, shall be forthcoming.) Individuals exist, by birth and circumstance, possessive of varying capacities which are not subject to equalization or moral engineering. Those capacities which are the result of natural endowments exist *in toto* and are resistant to manipulation, and hence not subject to moral redistribution, as much due to their immutability as because any such preposterous attempt would both deprive such advantaged persons unfairly of their characters and those less-advantaged dependents who are reliant upon their unique and needed skills. Fortunately, unequal anthropogenic or social circumstances are far more apt to moral engineering. Nevertheless, if fairness—the central virtue here articulated—is something we value, then it is ironic that it takes refuge in the hands of a race so seemingly averse to its realization.

There is no justice or injustice in nature, only in the kingdom of man. Quite simply, the realm of all morality exists solely within his purview, subsequent to the natural lottery of abilities. Hence, any formulation of moral imperatives must require his presence and response to the natural condition. While it is ever-noble to counter the amorality of nature, and a task man has met with considerable success, its omnipresent opposition to humanity's higher goals, coupled with our own inadequacies, inbuilt and contrived, makes its total decimation impossible. That is, we are inescapably prevented in ever achieving moral perfection, either individually or collectively, by virtue of our limitations and the overpowering unconquerability of nature. Any sensible ethics, especially one which prescribes a normative standard of argued moral perfection, must reflect both our inability to ever totally achieve it (while still striving to ceaselessly ever approach this goal, and to recognize the value in excellence if not perfection) and that we recognize when deference must be paid to those realities of nature which cannot be changed. We must *accept* that nature possesses an eternally superior strength by virtue of its omnipresence and infinite existence, and that the finiteness and frailty which marks our existence is no match for contention. Rather, the most we can attempt is a small step forward toward betterment, but one whose consequences still prove infinitely superior to the alternative of inaction. The goal of any moral theory, including the one to be presented, is not to achieve impossible leaps, but to make stronger and larger the smallish steps taken forward from the present.

Born from such a philosophical agenda as the above, meritocratic utilitarianism is an attempt to unify both the noblest aspirations of human ethics, namely justice, with the insurmountable natural barriers which prohibit its full entelechy. In this regard, it is a synthesis of the philosophical and the practical, the ideal and the real. This, I believe, to be one of its great strengths. Moreover, its new thesis will permit the unprecedented fusion of all major ethical theories (consequentialism, deontology and virtue ethics), the hedonic and stoic schools, an inclusion of considerations of justice absent from CU and the prescription of a universal moral law applicable and discernible in all scenarios, from the personal to the political.

We shall begin with MU's relation to CU. As each is a utilitarian theory, both advocate the maximization of pleasure. As already discussed, this is defensible by virtue of VMI. It does however, require additional explanation and justification. Utilitarian theories in general, whether MU, CU or any variant thereof, have a common virtue ensuring their supremacy as a moral framework: agent-neutrality. Whereas altruism and egoism initially unequally value the priorities of individuals, utilitarianism does not (however, to be discussed, MU does unequally value the priorities of individuals once additional information is known, unlike CU), instead adopting a third-person omniscient perspective independent of subjective bias. Moreover, it properly recognizes pleasure as valuable to *each* individual within a CF and that pleasure's maximization is most desirable from this impartial bird's-eye perspective, even if the bulk of the happiness delivered to this CF is unexperienceable by any one agent within said CF. In other words, utility maximization is a collective affair concerned with maximal numerical welfare over maximal individual welfare if the two conflict, for the latter occupies only a narrow scope of hedonic experience and enjoyment. For this reason, assuming no additional information, utilitarians prize the 'greater good.' We shall soon discover, however, that what indeed constitutes the greater good is many times counterintuitive to us, and requires a reversal in our traditional thinking.

What is this additional information so essential in transforming our moral thinking? As previously mentioned, utile resources are scarce, and thus must be prudently distributed. While one certainly prefers the absence of such restraints, the edicts of nature and social reality prevent such abundance. Simply, the criterion of judiciousness in utile resource allocation is *merit. Merit is the measure of the utility to* which *an individual/collective group* is entitled, *determined per the probability,*[1] *either formerly, presently or futurely, of his/its intentionally achieved utility output.* Because only the individual possesses agency, the scope of considerations of merit and accordant resource distribution usually refers to single actors, unless the calculation and provision of resources to so narrow a target prove infeasible or non-cost effective, in which case larger groups may be judged in terms of collective merit and provided for accordingly. Nevertheless, the concept of merit is simple: that a just distribution of utile resources is proportionate to the intended, achieved utility output of actors. Merit can operate presently, proactively and less often, retroactively. For example, when utile resources may be distributed virtually immediately after a worthy act (of whose existence and effects have a high if not certain probability of having occurred) has taken place, merit compensation occurs presently. Regarding future merit compensation, this is often seen on the predicted basis of potential worth (itself the payment/utility output legitimizing the required and initial entitlement to utile resources), perhaps the most obvious example being a scholarship or loan. A student of academic promise is preemptively provided funds

---

1 The probability referenced above is coincident with its usage as a term in statistics, and hence encompasses all strengths of belief, from unlikelihood to virtual certainty.

for study per the probability that he shall become a contributing member of society following his education; for scholarships, the benefit received diffusely by society is sufficient payment in return, while for loans its provider expects delayed yet direct compensation, often with interest—thus permitting his capacity to profit from the initial uncertain relinquishment of his money and its possible loss.

If there could exist an oversimplified mantra for MU, it would be as follows: what is moral is the intent, coupled with correspondent action, to seek '*the greatest happiness for the greatest producers* (of utility).' Because MU argues that resources and happiness should be allocated in the order of those who contribute most to the greatest happiness, then to those who are non-harmful, and lastly (if at all) to those who do harm, it conveys that goods and services be distributed from each according to his abilities, and to each according to his contribution. Resources should be distributed in order of utility production, as determined by a combination of both the quality of the pleasure produced and its quantity. When variant, quality ought be prioritized before quantity. When ascertainable, desert is based upon intent (which is usually assumed to correspond with action, unless evidence to the contrary arises), except in those situations in which compromise is necessary on a smaller level to ensure the equitable treatment of desert on a larger level. One common and clear example of this involves plea deals for unimportant thugs turning over evidence to convict a criminal kingpin. Such exceptions should only occur when reasonably unavoidable in pursuit of a greater good. Cumulatively, in MU we see a resplendently-unified whole; it incorporates elements of rule utilitarianism though permissive of overriding act utilitarian calculations in exceptional situations, recognizes the practicality of two-level moral judgment per reason (inclusive not simply of erudite and rationalized Benthamite calculations but also intuition, emotion and experiential assessment), that those traits which reflexively maximize this mantra (as found within virtue ethics and cultivated through the disciplined repetition of the above mandates) become automatized within our personalities, and the centrality of intent in determining moral desert of utile resources. Moreover, negative utilitarian concerns are addressed owing to the maximal efficiency with which the above principles ought to be conducted insofar as they seek maximal happiness, minimal unhappiness, and correspondently assume the dual benefits of both CU and negative utilitarianism. Lastly, perverse implications of misguided utilitarian thinking involving the pleasure gleaned from immoral behavior are excluded on the psychological basis that no properly-attuned mind could extract pleasure from behaving immorally, since the latter forfeits one's self-knowledge of desert of happiness, thereby forbidding its experience.

MU may be thought of as a 'downward spiral of resource provision,' beginning at the top with the greatest producers, descending in order of productivity. Any excess resources should be given to the zero-value producers as charity, if so willed by the productive, and only to negative 'utility vacuums' if for rehabilitative purposes (*e.g.*, criminals). This prioritization is not only morally sensible, but highly practical owing to the labor-intensiveness of resources and their subsequent scarcity. MU also respects individual freedoms and the vitality of self-improvement regarding jockeying for scarce resources, relying upon that most natural inclination of self-interest as the most efficient engine of both personal benefit and collective gain, rather than the contrivances of altruistic logic. Thus, merit is the lynchpin of desert because it is the most efficient, natural and sensible criterion to sustain utile output; its neglect would diminish any motivation toward the production of utility, and result in the abandonment of just reciprocity between contribution and its due reward.

Before furthering discussion on other matters, it is fruitful to examine hypothetical scenarios in which MU might be action-guiding, so as to understand more clearly its practical ramifications. Imagine, for instance, each of the following situations, themselves ranging from the extreme to the commonplace, all the while noting that the principles guiding appropriate action remain, not only universal, but omnipresently actionable:

An asteroid of mammoth size is hurtling toward the Earth, its collision imminent. Its impact shall obliterate all animal and plant life as we know it, thus ending all human civilization. There is sufficient room in a series of caves and mineshafts across the planet in which hundreds of thousands of survivors may live indefinitely—the result of advances in agronomics and high-technology. Assuming action shall be taken to save as many as possible, how ought selection for the few be carried out? Assuming the equality of individuals, the selection should be random, perhaps conducted by a computer sampling through citizenship records. This however, would be an unfortunate error of judgment. According to MU, selection should occur according to the merit and utility output of individuals. Since such a small number of individuals' lives are to be preserved, ensuring that those of the highest moral quality—as measured not only by their justness of behavior but their superior talents and their magnitudinous beneficial potential—are prioritized is paramount. Otherwise, the mean profile of one selected would exhibit mediocrity in every sense—hardly the standard with which one would wish to go forward in the repopulation of the world. Instead, engineers, botanists and scientists in general would be favored, as would farmers, a select few artists (all likely taken from the classical arts) and political leaders, administrators and jurists. Clearly, while saving all would be preferable, this forced choice requires us to view the individual value of each life as it exists in reality—differently.

A plane crashes on a deserted island and 100 people survive, trapped for a period no less than 4 years before managing to fashion a seafaring vessel with the intent to escape. Of this group, 20 are highly-meritorious, including an engineer, a doctor, a juridical scholar, a carpenter and an agronomist. The remaining 80 are manual laborers. Clearly, while all may be valuable in the collective enterprise of building a boat, there is little doubt that some are worth more than others in achieving this end. For example, while both the 'leaders' and 'laborers' are required as necessary utile classes in the construction of their ship, the loss of one member of the latter would be less negatively impactful than the loss of one of the former. This is not simply because there are more laborers than leaders, but because the net utility output of a given leader exceeds that of one laborer. For instance, whereas only one engineer may be required to design the vessel, dozens of men may be required to construct it. While the more abstruse professions may be considered a luxury, this is not so in the case of our scholar, for such a large group living together in otherwise isolation for so protracted a period of time requires common laws by which to abide. While MU supports these observations, it goes further regarding the division of goods. Assuming there exists an abundance of utility-producing resources (that is, beyond a bare minimum capable of sustaining each individual on the island), a truly morally appropriate distribution would not be one in which each member received an equal quantity (let us say of shells [a makeshift currency], wood, and size of dwelling). Instead, the leaders on the island ought to be allocated a greater portion of the goods, commensurate with their relative utility output, the reason being that the natural incentive to contribute their talents is diminished if they receive the same rewards as those whose labor is relatively less valuable (again assuming that neither the possibility of escape nor rescue is readily appreciable, and where the incentive to work in collaboration toward a common and viable goal does not exceed individual motivation toward just reward for personal labor). Not only would they suffer by virtue of inferior rewards, but so too would the collective, now lacking, in whole or in part, their vital energies and talents. The implications of this scenario are far ranging, and most obviously necessitate the inequalities evident within any large-scale economy, where respective utility output is the chief criterion of economic reward, for the worth of such output is most efficiently expressed through the valuations of free agencies exercised within a fundamentally unregulated market.

Imagine there to be a classroom of 30 schoolchildren. While 2 or 3 are troublemakers, the exceeding majority are mediocre and not noteworthy. One pupil stands out, however, and in a truly exceptional manner. Her unparalleled brilliance and rapidity of mind make her not simply the envy of her peers but an object of ill-deserved scorn. While the other students do not act upon their dislike of this wunderkind, they cannot help but feel cheated in not possessing the talents with which she was born. It cannot be said that she labors more tirelessly than her counterparts, for hers is the highest and most intuitive sense of genius— that which comes naturally and fluidly. Accordingly, time and time again, she receives the highest marks and wins a place at Cambridge. Should this not be the case, even if amongst her rank there are those who labor more acutely and protractedly? Should she not receive the benefits of her advantage, simply because it is inconvenient or saddening for those around her? Should she be forcibly equalized, dredging from her person the sole vestige of her uniqueness, much as her peers' distinctive shortcomings would too vaporize amongst the impersonality of their transformation into beings of complete indistinguishability from one another? Much as her talents cannot practically be subdivided and redistributed, to do so would diminish their powers for the greater good. If everyone were of identical intelligence, then what progress could be achieved, for no thought would be unthought, no idea original, to impel us in new directions of advancement? Thus, success is the result of tangible ability, not desired equality, and hence, subsequent to the realm of nature's lottery and resident instead within the domain of human behavior and the realization of disparate individual potential.

Clearly, the above situations constitute a defense of a conservative position. Society should cater to the 'best' (most vital to its optimal functioning) first, and then work its way downwards in terms of utile output. 'Best' is not determined by the vagaries of historical ancestry, but by personal merit and demonstrable ability. There is no merit in inherited nobility, only personal productivity, much as there is prestige only in utility. Prestige, in itself, is useless. As an interpersonal concept, it requires its bearers to become dependent upon the valuations of others; when doing so exceeds the absolute utility derivable only by the bearer, its pursuit is misguided. This is because it violates the supreme virtue of self-reliance, and calls upon one to invest his happiness in the whims of others; to have one's happiness live beyond the confines of his will, but rather dependently in the hands of others, is a severe blunder indeed. To covet thus all things beyond our will is equal folly predictive only of great sorrow.

The status of elites is not dependent upon caste or predetermined, but upon the character unique to every individual. This encourages self-reliance in the lower classes (determined chiefly by utility output, not necessarily financial health, but useful consumable commodity production), and through strength of character, this is almost always possible. It may be more difficult for the comparatively disadvantaged, but the alternative requires too much intervention to equalize circumstances which shall always prove to be unequal with each successive generation or within any given CF. Thus, the 'new aristocracy' of which we shall later discuss is the *meritocracy*—whose superior talents culminate in the greatest moral good being achieved, with the greatest efficiency, for the greatest number. No qualms shall be reticently shied away from in regards to what the precepts of this doctrine may necessitate. Social Darwinism is implied by such a position, as are potential practices as far-reaching and controversial as eugenics, forced neutering, and mating of the best to produce more of the best. Over time, however, these policies ought create a superior race where the mean is far higher (thus, maximizing our valuing of humanity in the long-term, rather than being squeamish about it in the short-term), the average man quite self-reliant. Such practices need not harm any weakened member in the present, but simply prioritize the stronger so that their capacities for success and achievement may be magnified contemporarily and multiplied intergenerationally. A heroic vision of the future, and one most people are too morally fearful and cowardly to implement. Our island plane crash example is important in showing the futility of attempting to rectify social inequalities—they shall always persist intra- and inter-generationally, naturally and socially—requiring constant third-party intervention, namely governmental. The lowest classes shall never be equal—it is contradictory to the spirit of both natural inequality and a capitalist respect for personal liberty, which is essential in aligning itself with human selfish nature, thus producing the utmost productivity per individual *and* collectively as well, as has been shown by social history, for collective gain is only permissible when meritorious individuals are free to progress both their own interests and those of their compatriots. No system of human hand may be perfect, but this is our best available option as evinced by history itself. Relatedly, there is seldom a quality as misunderstood and overvalued as modesty—the practice of contrived dishonesty so as to allay the justifiable insecurities of others. Neither humility nor hubris is an acceptable practice, but openness of recognition with oneself and his abilities—the accurate appraisal of our talents relative to others, and the subsequent assessment of our worth and confidence which should result. Such assessment is inevitable in the organization of labor and its valuation, and so, to hold a double standard in the marketplace and the social realm regarding how we value ourselves and advertise such value, is hypocritical, conjuring false hope in the minds of lessers that they are in fact their betters' equal.

Intent, Consequence and Negligence

How about intent? A man is stillborn if only of good intentions and a beast without them. In calculating and appropriately compensating merit, despite a preoccupation with outcome—that is, the tangible utility produced by actions—there also exists deep interest in the intent behind such actions. What ought that intent be, and how to verify it? Intuitively, we might ascribe virtually all moral weight upon one's intent, for it is only that which reveals the truth behind our actions. But is not this too, an asinine simplification? The answer, being yes, prompts us to further realize that while intentions are critical in revealing our sincerest attitudes toward a given situation and how we ought best respond to it in terms of action, they alone are insufficient in the practice of moral analysis. 'Tis too true that the consequences of an action alone, regardless of intent, leave the realm of moral judgment nothing more than a roulette wheel of reward and punishment, no agent responsible for his actions as a result of his lacked capacity for forethought. Nonetheless, the complete disregard of the consequences of an act similarly renders ethics an impotent science—one relegated to the realm of desire and not action, cause but not effect.

Good intentions do not make a good deed, but rather the latter is a result of a combination of the will and the body, *the intent and its corresponding action*. Framed in negative terms, this is analogous to the dual legal requirements of *mens rea* and *actus reus* being present in determining criminal culpability. Both the forethought inherent in intent and the tangible manifestation inherent in subsequent action are necessary for full moral judgment to occur—indeed, no choice itself may be claimed to be expressed unless constitutive of both components, and under conditions where one or more alternatives exist regarding courses we may pursue. If so, then ethicists are faced with a dilemma: assuming the necessity of these two components in the determination of an act's moral bearing, how are we to determine the relationship between motive and outcome? Presently, the answer proves less than satisfying.

Until that unfortunate day when privacy is an extinct relic of a gentler time crafted not by purer hearts so much as technological ignorance, and perfect information is made available regarding the truest thoughts of men, an event made possible only by the perverse intrusions of misguided science, it shall be impossible to know with anything greater than probability the allegiances of a man's conscience. Owing to this mulish obstacle, we have no choice but as reasonable men to assume that, except in cases whereby good evidence indicates contrarily, a man's actions are the result of a preceding, corresponding intent. Generally, we should affix to this rule of thumb the proviso that in times of palpable uncertainty, the defendant be provided the benefit of the doubt, for it seems a greater crime to punish the guiltless and produce clear harm, than to forgo the punishment of those guilty parties whose transgressions have already transpired and where achieving justice through punishment is, at best, unclear. In this sense, negative retributive justice is less pressing than the hijacking of hedonic desert out of the hands of the virtuous, whose greater priority to fair treatment follows from their increased concern for such values in the first place, and their heightened worthiness to avoid ill-treatment.

Moreover, we can recognize that there lives a greater good in avoiding uncertainly-deserved suffering (a form of relative pleasure) than in providing its certain due (a form of relative displeasure); pleasure as the only good mandates that its provision (even if in the guise of the absence of uncertainly-deserved punishment) be prioritized above that of its opposite manifestation, certainly-created pain. Justice for utility engines must by virtue of their superior output take priority over the withholding of utile resources from utility vacuums, themselves unworthy to reap them by virtue of the inferior offspring of their acts. Equally important, it is more practical and utility-efficient to postpone retribution rather than preemptively practice it, and perhaps irreversibly, punish the potentially innocent, for pursuant to such knowledge, utility-intensive rectification is often required, and may be unable to perfectly restore or compensate for the prior hedonic *status quo*.

What of the disparate value of intent versus consequence? In this matter, the answers are straightforward. Consequences are ultimately more morally important than intentions, for only the former may be tangibly experienced, and the latter only manifested through them. Moreover, in terms of judgment, consequences are fairly simple to measure, whereas intent is not; thus, the former is often the most reliable means available to us in judging character. Further, in situations involving the greater good as otherwise compromised against an impure intent (*e.g.*, using von Braun's mind to launch the space program versus his use of wartime slave labor), the greatest beneficial consequence (when deserved by a greater number than those undeservingly benefitting from good fortune by virtue of their necessity, such as von Braun) must trump the minority's unpunished immorality. Intent is significant insofar as it determines *desired consequences*, thus serving as an instrument measuring moral desert. Moral luck plays no valid role in the determination of such desert. Whereas MU stipulates desert is a function of *intended consequences*, and hence intent, such is practicably achieved only through observation of outward behaviors and their consequences. If perfect knowledge of the mind could be had, *intent as intended consequences* would be the criterion for worthiness of happiness, independent of the actual consequences which arose (assuming such intent was manifested via action, however successful, and non-negligent, as to be discussed).

Lastly in our discussions of intent, the astute observer might recognize the problematic vacuity left by negligence. In understanding that both intent and correspondent action are necessary in the analysis of an act's moral bearing, in what capacity may we assess negligence as a coaxial consideration? We learn, perhaps unexpectedly, that negligence falls squarely into both camps, for to *act* sloppily unfortunately only *appears* a more endemic misfortune than to think so. *Negligence, therefore, is the deliberately active or passive failure to adequately concern oneself with the consequences of his actions, at any point in time from intent formation to execution to act completion, which ultimately results in the hedonic inefficiency of the consequences of an act.* Negligence is therefore, a weakly immoral act, insofar as it entails the necessarily foresighted failure to appropriately pay due diligence to the consequences of one's actions, whether significant or trifling. Clearly, the dangers inherent in negligence, as well as its moral objectionability, are directly proportional to the potential gravity of those actions and their consequences to which it affects. In the case of negligence leading to unexpected benefits, no moral praise is to be awarded the actor, but instead the same admonition as to be expected assuming the worst case scenario per his negligence. Of course, as good sense dictates, that which is beyond the reasonable control of one to foresee or control and which may lead to unintentionally disfavored consequences, is beyond the consideration of negligence, and may be attributed to bad luck, devoid of moral fault.

Omission

There are only two sins: to do harm, and to not do good. Omission is potential wasted or misdirected. It is thusly a knotty poser for moral philosophers, especially those of the deontological variety. The reason being that while omission is, at times, seemingly preferable to harmful action, it too can prove equally troubling when it results in unfortunate consequences. Take, for example, Foot's classic trolley problem. Here, the issue of whether to positively interfere in the ongoing course of a runaway trolley bound to kill several people is counterbalanced by the equally-undesirable task of having to, in the process of actively diverting it, kill a single individual on another platform. For the deontologists, the answer is clear (assuming, indeed, that the principle upheld is the impermissibility of taking a life): do nothing, and let the trolley crash into the more populated platform, killing loads more people. They will claim that, while this outcome is indeed unfortunate, one's omission is the only guarantor of obedience to the aforesaid deontological proscription on killing, and that this inaction is essential in permitting there to be an 'out' in every conceivable scenario under a deontological system. Otherwise, if both failing to redirect the trolley and not doing so would predictably kill people, and killing was absolutely forbidden, our agent would have been placed in the unenviable position of having no morally-permissible choice. This implies that there are certain zugzwangs under which no moral options exist, but only lesser and inescapable evils—a horrid thought to ethicists and escape-artists alike. If one approaches this problem at this particular angle, the deontologists are correct; that is, omission clearly has to be taken as a morally-permissible course of 'inactive action.' It fails however to prove a convincing position, for two key reasons.

First, omission is qualitatively identical to a positive action; it possesses both intent and tangible consequences. Because of this, to classify omission as a special class of action, one excused from normal moral considerations, is self-deluded. This is clear because omission, *like all deontological rules*, is only desirable because it achieves some consequence. Hence, deontology collapses into a form of consequentialism, for even the most intuitive inherent moral laws are only valuable not in the abstract, but because they achieve some end which is sensibly beneficial to us. Hence, omission is no different; it either attempts to achieve some end by adherence to an abstract principle, or because it plainly attempts to prevent some tangible harm.

Second, the concept that certain actions are inherently, and thus, universally, moral or immoral requires us to descend into the realm of metaphysical folly. While later attention will be paid to this particular topic, deontological claims regarding certain intrinsic moral properties which exist in nature are as counterintuitive as they are untrue. Moreover, they fail to take into account the notion of *circumstantial preferentiation*—that is, the relative value ascribed to certain preferences dependent upon one's place amid a given situation. Because preferences clearly adapt to one's circumstances (*e.g.*, while we might normally value gold bullion above a canteen of water, we might appraise things differently if in the Sahara), it is abominably obstinate to disregard the relative values of dissimilar actions and their distinct consequences.

Consequently, omission of action is an invalid concept; all choices are the result of intention and correspondent fulfillment of that intention, whether with positive action or negative refrainment. Therefore, all omission, as intended inaction, is itself an action—it possesses the required elements of intent and correspondent fulfillment, whether positive or negative. The end result is an insoluble problem for deontologists—unlike utilitarians, who deal in matters of preferentially relative and not absolute courses of action—in that the inexistence of omission as a coherent behavioral concept makes impossible their occasionally mandated abstinence from all possible courses of nominally-immoral action within a given scenario, providing no moral guidance in particular scenarios. Hence, this lacuna is illustrative of the unique flaw of deontology in its erroneous and untenable construction of universal behavioral prescriptions.

Quantifying Pleasure

A key obstacle for meritocratic utilitarians is the quantification of competing hedonic priorities. That is, whose interests are more pressing: those of the industrialist responsible for running a massive factory (and hence overseeing many workers) or a single employee? Cursorily assuming the former, the question becomes both more significant and perplexing when calculating the relative interests of the industrialist and *all* his employees—which is greater now? Inevitably imperfect knowledge of the situation proves this to be a perennial conundrum. In this case, without necessary further analysis, most would intuitively conclude the latter by sheer number. These problems of quantification shall herein be explored, per both the number affected and to what degree, the latter being determined via the hedonic metrics of *intensity, purity, duration* and *quality*, the last of which refers to the hierarchy of pleasures.

To briefly define, each of these pleasure-related metrics, known as *Proper Hedonic Metrics*, can be understood as follows:

Intensity – the magnitude and strength of the pleasure being experienced, the minimal value of which is the smallest possible sensory or cognitive experiential threshold, alternatively known as the *liminal threshold*

Purity – the extent to which the pleasure being experienced is combined with contrary experiences—that is, painful ones—of any intensity

Duration – the temporal period during which the pleasure is experienced

Quality – the most difficult to quantify, this metric refers to a pleasure's correspondent place on the Hierarchy of Pleasures; namely, its existence as a principally physical, emotional or intellectual pleasure, whereby each successive type is of increasing hedonic value

Additionally, in quantifying the relative hedonic desirability of one course of action over another, the probability of success is a critical factor, and to this extent, *likelihood* can be added to the list of pleasure-related factors which need be taken into account when quantifying an action's potential moral worth. Likelihood, in this regard, ought not only take into account the probability of achieving the given hedonic end, but also said act's own consequences, confined to a suitable foreseeability as only reason dictates, such as regarding whether the achievement of action X to achieve hedonic end Y shall be likely to subsequently yield the easier experience of Y in future circumstances (reproducibility), or if it will make the further experience of Y more difficult or equally so (infertility). It, along with *population*, does not refer to the nature of the pleasure itself, unlike the above four metrics, but rather, its practicable impact; consequently, these factors are titled *Semi-Hedonic Metrics*. A third non-pleasure-related factor exists, and that is *immediacy*, or simply, the duration before the pleasure can be experienced. With due deference, it should be noted that the above calculus is essentially identical to the one first pioneered by Bentham.

Thus, in summary, the entire list of quantifiable traits of an act which must be assessed, along with the pleasure to be emitted, are as follows: *intensity, purity, duration, quality, population, likelihood* (of act X's hedonic success and its potential offspring) and *immediacy*. As the astute observer shall note, these seven characteristics correspond to a quadaxial framework: *experience* (intensity, purity, quality), *chronology* (duration, immediacy), *extent* (number affected/population) and *probability* (likelihood). As previously discussed, while numeration is extremely difficult, it corresponds not to an absolute scale, but rather one whose values are determined by relative comparisons between potential courses of action, their natures and outcomes, as measured by each one of these hedonic metrics.

Efficiency

One of the most commonplace—and legitimate—objections to utilitarians is the concept of efficiency. Alright, the deontologist may temporarily concede, it is acceptable to kill (for killing is always seemingly the immediate utilitarian aim!) 1 for a 1,000, but what about 1 for 100, for 10...for 2? At what point will the endangered respect for individuals mean so little that utilitarianism is merely a game of gruesome calculation? Much as utilitarianism possesses a weakness regarding the problem of calculating utilities, no doubt its tendency toward sliding down that slippery slope of bloodlust for the greater good appears far keener than its deontological counterpart. Nevertheless, the utility of an idea or activity must seldom if ever be proscribed for fear that its abuse, and not inherent nature, may lead to unfortunate outcomes. The same holds true in this case; efficiency is the ultimate safeguard which ensures that utilitarian sacrifices are conducted in the most humane and economical manner. Considering the alternative would be the failure to respect the rights of a larger majority (numerically) or superior utility source (meritwise) in the adherence to deontological principles, the risk associated with attempting to most austerely obey the principles of utilitarian sacrificial calculations suddenly appears relatively desirable, assuming of course we exclude those conceivable and rare instances in which such utilitarian sacrifice may plausibly lead to their abuse. While strict rule utilitarians and deontologists will attempt to flay this subtle exception mercilessly as a mortal vulnerability, they fail to realize that such abused scenarios are in fact quite rare, and that while the concept of rule utility is sound, it falls apart when genuinely meritorious and exceptional situations arise which require either paralysis of action in its wake or adaptability, itself the only viable option. It is efficiency and conservative cautiousness which render the latter course of action not only palatable, but necessary. For, what defines an extreme action versus a reasonable one, save the circumstances? Any man of sound judgment must be prepared to act according to his setting.

Benevolent Equity

Benevolent Equity (BE) has been perhaps the single most consistent element of my moral philosophy throughout the years, save for my strict adherence to hedonism. In short, BE is the concept that there are twin pillars of moral behavior: first and foremost there is equity, or reciprocal justness of one's actions per both intent and magnitude, and secondly benevolence, or the provision of undeserved utility. Whereas equity corresponds with justice and is hence absolute and uniaxial, benevolence is biaxial, concerned with either the undeserved provision of pleasure to others (also known as *charity*, or *positive benevolence*) or the deliberate refrain from delivering due punishment or pain (also known as *mercy*, or *negative benevolence*).

Equity is necessarily an interpersonal phenomenon since a response to the actions of others, whereas benevolence may be applied either interpersonally or toward oneself through the act of forgiveness of those transgressions which do not threaten moral fundamentality. While equity represents the normative ideal and chief priority of moral matters, benevolence is critical in the practical daily functionings of people, owing to their inherent tendency toward imperfection and laxness in obeying unbending rules. Accordingly, benevolence is required to accept the human nature as it is—that is, deviant from any prescribed and absolute rule by which to ever-follow. Moreover, benevolence is the purest form of moral behavior, done because it constitutes provision of pleasure—one intrinsic good—and forgiveness of acceptable imperfection, another optional, though recognizable good. The knowledge of this purely good act, independent from the self-interested concerns of reciprocity as found in justice, permits it to serve as a means of self-directed pleasure (in addition to the more obvious aid brought to another) in the sense that its knowledge of execution justifies our own moral desert of happiness, whereby such desert is created intellectually, informing us that we may deserve to then further pursue pleasure (of any form) as a resultant reward of such known prerequisite desert, and independently of the pleasing knowledge such desert itself also brings.

In short, BE lends credence to the notion that morality consists minimally of justice, and maximally of charity. Absolute equity is the minimal and only obligatory moral standard of behavior. That is, to give no more than is to be received, and accept no more than to be equally paid, either then or soon after. Thus, a well-fed man may in clear (albeit unpraiseworthy) conscience deny a starving fellow who has provided him no benefit his unneeded food, so long as he remains certain that if the roles were reversed, and he were the starving man, he would sincerely waive any demand for such charity. Similarly, he who benefits from such munificence must too be wholly willing to repay such charity, the goal to convert it into an act of repaid kindness, and hence justice, rather than allow it to remain benevolence.

Here, charity is praiseworthy not because it approximates justice, but because its practitioner recognizes the innate desirability of utility and directing it toward the enjoyment of others, and correspondingly gleans a sense of moral desert of happiness from doing such good. It is because all men are flawed that charity is permissible, and exists within that scope of acceptable practice spanning from moral sufficiency to excellence which may characterize a man's moral constitution. For, if men were perfectly just, then charity would not only be unnecessary but positively immoral, since it would be an example of mercy toward the unworthy and an excessive burden upon the virtuous. Only in failure is our humanity revealed. Benevolence is thus the tolerance of acceptable imperfection in men. To be excellent requires courage; to be good and imperfect requires more.

MU and BE complement each other, as found most especially in regard to equity; MU argues that utility provision must match utility output—here, a clear example of equity at work. Moreover, the hierarchy of pleasures as reflected in utility distribution not per numerical maximization but rather the greatest producers of the greatest quality of pleasure (in qualitative descending order, then followed by quantitative descending order) is illustrative that what is justly due regarding utility output must take into account the intrinsic quality of said utility. In this regard, MU may be understood as a more nuanced formulation of BE, and what constitutes justness between utility engines, as regards consideration for quality, as well as quantity of output. There is nothing of value beyond the experienceable. Hence, quality must be prioritized before quantity, for the latter is far less related to the direct nature of personal experience.

Benevolence, however, also enters into the MU framework; regarding ecopolitical systems, whereas MU would necessarily advocate a fairly *laissez-faire* free market with limited governmental regulation, which, assuming true freedom of agency (at least in the negative sense) existed among all actors would ensure the existence of equity, benevolence would be encouraged insofar as social programs were in place which ensured fundamental intergenerational equality of opportunity, thereby likely minimally requiring the emergence of juvenile education and healthcare, for there is no self-sufficiency without either of these social goods. Similarly, such a necessarily mildly-redistributive economy would cater to the elderly through pay-as-you-go pension schemes and housing for the *involuntarily non-autonomous* (INA), such as the mentally handicapped—those segments of the population whose utility output is suboptimal or inexistent through no fault of their own. Such actions are therefore to be considered charitable or benevolent, as opposed to strictly equitable. On a micro-interpersonal level, benevolence might involve the encouraged giving to charity among the affluent because of their presumed understanding of such actions to be both intrinsically good owing to their capacity for utility production, but moreover because of the realization that enjoyment of said utile resources would be heightened among the needy owing to the greater scarcity of such utility amongst them, whereby the relative value of given utile resources is in part a function of their scarcity.

Encouragement of such altruism often exists in the form of tax deductions, and is encouraged not because mandatory, but because known to be an intrinsic good—the same reasoning for why partial charitable initiatives should be taken on by the government. Such promote a sense of unity within society, neither so collectivized as to nebulize personal identity and stave ambition, nor so atomized as to wholly alienate the individual. Here, even though the affluent presumably 'deserve' such greater utility, they would still be encouraged, though not mandated, to behave charitably. On an intrapersonal MU level, a meritorious high school student awarded a scholarship to a prestigious university ought still accept, even if he knows himself to have received slightly lower test scores than another rejected applicant (*ceteris paribus*), because to not do so would represent a failure to accept negligible imperfections in the nature of a meritocratic system; in this regard, he would behave benevolently toward himself, and accept the benefits of a university place he did not precisely—but still overall—deserved. As evident, both MU and BE apply to all spheres of human interaction—from the macroscopically interpersonal or political to the self-regarding intrapersonal.

Morality equaling benevolent equity, or formulized as M = BE, is herein argued to be the most powerful ethical equation ever devised. It perfectly encapsulates the edicts of meritocratic utilitarianism above, prioritizing mandatory, morally-baseline equity but allowing room for optional charity—recognizing that maximizing hedonic provision is itself a good because pleasure is the good, and that pardoning those of non-fundamental imperfection is inherently reasonable and thus desirable. Both benevolence (B) and equity (E) refer to the allocation of pleasure, either in the positive provision of it or the relative alleviation of pain, thus increasing the former. Just as there exists a hierarchy of pleasures, so too can this be inbuilt into the equation, whereby hedonic prioritization is taken into account in the pursuit of justice and charity, and whereby maximizing the efficiency with which all pleasures may be experienced constitutes maximal obedience to the equation's edicts. In summary, to be moral is to act equitably with oneself and others in terms of the provision of pleasure, with the preferable option of further providing limited pleasure to an undeserving self and others, or, acting charitably.

The Universal Moral Law

In this section, I shall formulate the aforementioned principles into a single, unified law. It shall incorporate elements of both meritocratic utilitarianism and benevolent equity, and be presented in two formulations in increasing levels of complexity and qualification.

I find it appropriate, however, so as to expedite conceptual grasping, that an extremely cursory distillation shall be presented at the outset:

> 'That which is moral requires the intended act to establish equity—the balancing of the hierarchical utile natures of those actions between parties—and to a lesser, optional extent, the establishment of benevolence—or undeserved charity—whereby individual autonomy is held to be fundamentally sovereign unless such respect violates equity.'

Thusly, morality is fundamentally constitutive of the doctrine of benevolent equity combined with the understanding that equity, and its appropriate due distribution of utile resources, is in accordance with the hierarchy of pleasure which underpins the rationale of meritocratic utilitarianism, which prioritizes such distribution on the principal basis of the qualitative superiority of pleasures, and secondarily, their quantitative maximization.

Universal Moral Law (UML) 1 – Shorthand Definition

a) 'That which is morally required is that which produces, by virtue of premeditated non-negligent intent and reasonability, the greatest qualitative happiness for the greatest number, whereby utility provision to any individual is proportionate to his best known already-existent or projected utility production (as determined first by the nature of the intent behind such production and the robustness of its attempted manifestation, successful or not; secondly its quality, and then thirdly by its quantitative impact).' This assumes utility-producing resources possess equal impact for all; if this is untrue, then affecting a greater number with a lesser-quality utility becomes permissible, if such resources are more impactful to this group. This is a general rule; calculating it beyond this precision becomes very difficult and contestable.

b) 'Utility provision directed toward one or more individuals such that it is greater than their generated utility production, is charitable, morally preferable to a), but not required.'

c) 'Respect for personal autonomy must exist so long as compatible with the aforementioned provisions (particularly as concerns the primacy of achieving equity), whose priority is prior to autonomy when the two classes conflict.'

d) 'The converse of these provisions collectively is immoral, and there exists a direct proportion between the decreasing efficiency with which these mandates are executed from a supposed initial perfect efficiency and the decreasing moral purity of the act. When impossible to fully achieve all these provisions within a given contextual frame, the imperative is to adhere to their mandates with as great efficiency as possible; in such instances, the reasonable incapability to perform these provisions at perfect efficiency is excusable (assuming this incapability is not the result of negligence, but unforeseeability), when it results from diminished or inexistent free will, whose maximal exercise, even if suboptimal, may still ensure the greatest fidelity to the above possible, and hence constitute the most moral action possible in given circumstances when they themselves dictate moral perfection impossible. Such circumstantial constraints do not themselves diminish the moral content of one's actions; only one's capacity to perform them to the utmost made jointly possible by his will and circumstantial restraints, if any exist, define the moral content of such actions.'

UML 2 – Formal Definition

'That which is moral is that which produces, via singular act or consistent personality trait, by virtue of premeditated non-negligent intent and reasonability, firstly, the greatest qualitative happiness for the greatest number, in descending order of hedonic quality affecting the greatest number within a given contextual frame (assuming that happiness-producing resources and/or actions for the highest-qualitative happiness producers would equally impact lesser-qualitative happiness producers; otherwise, a greater number of the latter class would take precedent if such resources would prove more impactful to them, whereby the number required for this exception is calculable with high, albeit imperfect, accuracy, and dependent on the relative value of the higher pleasure sacrificed in the former group as compared with various other pleasures, above [if possible] and below it, along the continuum of all possible pleasures [taking into account their intensity, quality, duration, purity, numerical impact, likelihood, and immediacy]; moreover, there are bounded thresholds to this principle: one may not permissibly completely sacrifice the highest-qualitative happiness-producers for a greater number of lesser-qualitative happiness producers in a given contextual frame because an inviolably valuable hedonic species would become lost, and likewise one is obligated to sacrifice a few higher-qualitative happiness-producers for a greater number of lesser ones within a given contextual frame because short of such a higher quality of happiness becoming extinct the greatest numerical experience of pleasure, even if of lower form, takes precedent), whereby utility provision to any individual is proportionate to his best known already-existent or projected utility production (as determined by the above prioritization, and assuming the nature of the intent behind such production is moral as herein defined, and its attempted manifestation, whether successful or not, is sufficiently robust) enjoyed by receiving actors; secondly and optionally, though still preferably in certain situations requiring personal judgment, itself morally-bound to a standard of reasonability permitting only a negligible degree of freedom from the moral objectivity herein this Law, utility provision directed toward one or more individuals (whether personally enjoyed or not) such that it is greater than their generated utility production; respect for personal autonomy must exist so long as compatible with the aforementioned provisions (particularly as concerns the primacy of achieving equity), whose priority is prior to autonomy when the two classes conflict; the converse of these provisions collectively is immoral, and there exists a direct proportion between the decreasing efficiency with which these mandates are executed (which includes acts of omission which either entirely violate their prescription or minimize their efficiency) from a supposed initial perfect efficiency and the decreasing moral purity of the act at hand; moreover, and when impossible to fully achieve all these provisions within a given contextual frame, the imperative is to adhere to their mandates with as great efficiency as possible; in such instances, the reasonable incapability to perform these provisions at perfect efficiency is excusable (assuming this incapability is not the result of negligence, but unforeseeability), when it results from diminished or inexistent free will, whose maximal exercise, even if suboptimal, may still ensure the greatest fidelity to the above possible, and hence constitute the most moral action possible in given circumstances when they themselves dictate moral perfection impossible; such circumstantial constraints do not themselves diminish the moral content of one's actions; only one's capacity to perform them to the utmost made jointly possible by his will and circumstantial restraints, if any exist, define the moral content of such actions.'

What are the implications of these morally-binding rules? They are extensive and deep. Among the most prominent include that just actions, or those which equitably transfer utility between agents, are preferable to charitable ones, which themselves, though desirable, are morally unmandated and relatively less moral than the alternative of justice. By definition, charity requires 'undeserved' utility provision; that is, in consequentialist terms, whereby hedonic input received by Agent A exceeds his hedonic output. A would thus be said to be the recipient of charity. When charitable actions are performed, it is thus preferable that those at least partially worthy of their received utility take priority above those wholly unworthy of it, the inactive themselves prioritized over the negatively utile—who, if fundamentally so (rather than only within a confined contextual frame), deserve no charity at all.

Another issue is the idea of liminal thresholds. How far ought one to be rewarded for his actions if they are only impactful to an ultra-negligible level—the smallest experienceable one—known as the *liminal threshold*? The answer is, expectedly, minimally—to the same extent as the net utility of his actions for all those affected. Similarly, should he be encouraged to contribute in this minimal form to the greater number, or more significantly to a fewer? There is no silver bullet in answering these questions, but owing to the extreme negligibility of this matter, a more significant contribution to a smaller number is generally advisable.

Moreover, while these laws indicate the criticality of intent in the moral assessment of individuals, there is a similarly august emphasis placed upon the consequences of their actions. Why? The answer being that maximizing the beneficial and tangible consequences of one's actions is a chief priority for the moral agent, for the fruits of his labors are only experienceable through such earthy consequences as opposed to strict adherence to ethereal deontological principles otherwise without effect. Meanwhile, moral judgment is a duality of assessing both intent and its requisite efficacy in achieving tangible and good ends, as defined by the above UML. Moreover, mandates of the UML are confined within the boundaries of reasonable behavior, despite calls for fundamental objectivity on the part of actors when assessing hedonic prioritization (per the aforementioned hierarchy of pleasures) and hence the course their actions ought to take. Hence, our moral procedure is as follows: 1) form an intent to achieve a calculated projected utility, maximizing the quantity of the highest available quality pleasure, and 2) act correspondently toward that intent.

Additionally, there is the issue of desert. Who, and how, are we exactly worthy of our received utility? Is worthiness a function of output, of intent, of simply effort? The answer lies, ultimately, in the first two: output and intent, for reasons both philosophical and practical. While effort is certainly commendable (*e.g.*, one cannot help but root for the struggling underdog, however hopeless his chances against the indomitable foe who makes light work of his defeat), it is not generative of the utility necessary in beneficial tangible experience. Accordingly, while it may not be fair that the talented are more capable and productive, such is largely beyond the concern of human justice, when the result of their emergence from a natural aristocracy. Only the realm of the influenceable and affectable belongs to human concerns for justice. While those which are the result of undeserved social inequality persist, the eradication of this phenomenon is never to be fully extinguished either, though the proper valuation of merit as a criterion for desert ought to heavily ameliorate this rectifiable wrong. Nonetheless, in the final analysis it is output which is critical, as is correspondent moral intent behind its creation. While this is thus far largely unknowable, it is a non-issue for we may look to the consequences of one's behavior as the likeliest indicator of his motives. While this is practical, desert per output is also philosophically sound, for so long as the talented capable of greatest output (say, by virtue of superior intelligence or inculcated work ethic, the result of being born into a good environment) persist with pure intent, it is unfair to reward them any less than those less-able who must toil greater to achieve equal or lesser results. To reward all groups equally, regardless of output, disregards the fundamental incentivization necessary for the highest-performing to continue as they were, rather than labor less and receive the same bounties as those less talented, thereby simultaneously disadvantaging the collective of their superior contributions. In this regard, there is a blind spot which can never be made wholly just, owing to the inextricable inequality of man. No moral or eugenic engineering may ever eradicate such disparities, for even the most improved of us in the present, if suddenly the future norm through evolution, would quickly become themselves the underclass of a new and subsequently improved subspecies.

The UML however extends beyond the ostensible boundaries of moral prescriptions insofar as they relate solely to interpersonal relations. I speak of course, of the ecopolitical—that intersection between economics and politics necessary in the organization of society. While it shall be greatly expanded subsequently, the UML posits a fundamentally conservative position economically, whilst a liberal one socially. The secularization of society is inevitable, the inexorable triumph of the appeal of reason in the minds of men over unreasoned traditions. The social issues are dead; what shall remain are only economic ones.

While the UML thus coincides with a broadly libertarian philosophy, it does so for very different reasons and at times, finds itself diametrically opposed to the former's prescriptions (such as regards conscription, which it may find necessary in times of unavoidable war because of the utilitarian mandate to protect society). While libertarianism prioritizes individual liberty, the UML places utility at the center of its axiology, recognizing that desert of utile resources is a far more pressing matter than tolerance of disparate behaviors and lifestyles (an issue largely unconnected with the more urgent former). This law requires that since utile resources are scarce, and their distribution should reflect individual utility production, a conservative economic policy ought to follow. It is one which greatly encourages economic self-reliance in pursuit of each individual becoming a 'utility engine,' the ultimate Equiist moral and economic end. For, it is self-reliance which makes moral action possible. As all moral action reduces to utility production, one cannot provide utile resources toward others unless self-reliant himself; instead, one represents the highest indignity of existing as a utility vacuum and thriving only on the optional charity of others. Whereas economic goods should first be distributed per individual productivity, what remains, if any, of utile resources should be allocated to those sections of society labeled as the INA. Again, such action is viewed as benevolent, rather than wholly just. Contrarily, it recognizes that social structures—whether concrete or ideological—based upon foundations other than reason must be dispatched in favor of those which encourage a tripartite maximization of liberty, security and utility. Accordingly, matters such as individual lifestyle choices or religion should not influence public policy, for they are not matters relevant to the ecopolitical priorities just referenced. Rather, They exist within the private sphere.

The Equiist UML is unique insofar as it combines a deontological respect for the individual, as revealed in its valuing his unfungibility when his high merit is present and unique, with the understanding that utilitarian calculations are necessary when satisfaction of all interests is impossible. By extension of its principles, those interests which must be first sacrificed are those which achieve the lowest utility, assuming that the magnitude of the impact of such utility is equal to that of higher forms. Thus, whereas opera is clearly more highly utile than food, if there were only one hunter and one opera singer among a dozen castaways, clearly the hunter would be more prized, as in this case the lower utile good is more impactful—more necessary for continued functioning—than the opera singer. *Ceteris paribus*, however, and assuming food were not in short supply, the opera singer's moral interests ought to take priority. These same considerations must be taken into account involving the State's role in managing the competing interests of citizens, such as their

conscription in times of just and unavoidable war, where, for instance, a higher-utile producer ought be exempt before a lower-
one, such as in the case of college deferments.

Those agents who practice the UML are collectively referred
to as the New Aristocracy, its characteristics discussed below.

The New Aristocracy

What is the New Aristocracy? Their conceptualization and
reinvention has occurred multiple times throughout history, in
forms as diverse as their geographic expanse and as ambitious as
the underlying motives of their precipitation. Simply, the New
Aristocracy (NA) is that body of men and women who make society not just possible, but worthwhile. It is a truism that society
arose so as to provide mutual protection between agents, and
that in doing so, a portion of each one's liberties had to be for-
feited. This implies, correctly, that the legitimate basis of society
was to increase the potential utility attainable by the individual, beyond that accessible in his prior state of nature. Accordingly, in addition to a macroscopic approach, society must be
a good on a microscopic—individual—level. However, in order
to achieve a stable social construct, certain institutions must be
in place: a robust military, basic civic services, a legislature and
domestic protection against infractions such as aggression and
contractual fraud, protection itself divided into two branches of
enforcement and a judiciary.

There is however, an important omission. In every society,
from its inception to extinction, there has always existed a hierarchy of individuals stratified by a variety of criteria, ranging from wealth to physical appearance to sex. Throughout the
centuries however, there has only existed one true criterion
for stratification, and it is ultimately this one, upon which the
strength of any body politic stands: the individual merits of its
citizenry. Whether the Alhambra Decree resultant in the intellectual and eventual 17th-century economic decline of Spain to
the American practice of slavery which detonated into a catastrophic civil war to the turbulence of the modern suffragette
movement to even the life-devaluing collectivism of communist
Russia, the denial not of utility itself, but the *freedom* to produce

utility with due compensation has been the clearest harbinger of societal strife and, ultimately, collapse. The reason being that in the final analysis, the protection and encouragement of merit is the key to optimal social functioning; it, like a law of physics, is unpervertable without horrendous consequence, and remains so despite the charade of man-made legislation, rules or the mores of any particular era. Hence, the only glue which makes possible the stability and future progress of a culture, race or individual—is merit.

The word aristocracy comes from the Greek *aristokratia*, 'rule of the best.' Abstractly, this corresponds with the idea that society ought to be governed by those individuals replete with the highest privileges not of economic wealth, but moral character and talent. In this regard, owing to their unique capacity for superior utile output, NAs ultimately rule in moral matters. It is this idea which Equiism wholeheartedly adopts, and not any historical etymological corruption predicated upon the idea that mere socioeconomic status, itself an artifact of birth and not personal industry, is the benchmark of aristocratic right to rule. Accordingly, it is this original, albeit now newfound, aristocracy of which we shall speak.

Whether labeled as the bourgeoisie, that dependable middle-class possessive of a Protestant work ethic or the glorious ascent of the self-made man, the New Aristocracy is seldom an innovative idea in itself—how many depictions in history or popular media which portray the *homo novus* or the supposed vulgarity of the *nouveau riche contra* the intrinsic social superiority of the old order, or the frustrated young lad on scholarship unaccepted by his legacy peers at university, testify to associated disconcerting trends! In an era where we allegedly value merit above all things, there still remains that fascination for a social hierarchy dependent upon historical inertia and the inherent human prejudice of assigning rankings to individuals. Such is why we still revel in the pageantry of a royal wedding or modify our behavior if in the presence of a titled nobleman, whose only superiority rests in the realm of good luck. People, in general, are attracted to the appeal of a social hierarchy, so long as it is unoppressive to them specifically. It is a source of cultural and social pride, stability and tradition—mainstays which are valued because of their capacity in providing a shorthand toward personal identification, itself felt necessary so as to classify and categorize the diverse spectrum which typifies the human race, for where there is diversity, there is the human need to dominate and polarize, separate and conquer. Nonetheless, history has revealed that these latter trends proved the seeds of their own destruction; despite their lengthy run, they were no match for the numerical superiority of their victims; hence has been the logistical rationale behind the intellectual acceptance of the meritocracy. It is one of the great fortunes of our time that this trend was, whether genuine or the auspicious accident of Grub Street intellectuals defending self-interest, in fact aligned with the auspices of reason, and philosophically sound.

According to the UML, the utilitarian distribution of goods should not be based on a mere nod to numbers, but rather, the quality of those individuals affected. Perhaps this is the ultimate encapsulation of the mantra, 'quality, not quantity.' Assuming utile resources are equally deserved and beneficial to various groups, higher-quality pleasures' distribution must take precedent owing to their intrinsically superior nature. Thus, Equism adopts a Millian view of there existing a hierarchy of pleasures—one defined not so much by the austere computations of Bentham, but upon a relative continuum which appeals to the higher or lower senses of man. It is the view of this treatise that those individuals who collectively endeavor to pursue and produce the greatest quality of utility are the explicit New Aristocracy, and that those who by virtue of their utility output are net providers, and hence self-reliant, the implicit New Aristocracy, insofar as quantity of utility becomes the primary criterion for their inclusion. An aristocracy not by blood, but virtuous choice and productivity. The notion of an aristocracy is perfectly valid, both natural and socially required. Its historical conception, however, is deeply misguided. To claim superiority by birthright is nonsensical; rather, an aristocrat is one who, being best apt to govern, first himself and then others, requires only one vital quality: a commitment to self-reliance and moral behavior, followed by the discretionary though often inevitable cultivation of superior tastes and activities, themselves a reflection of the highest class of pleasures—to be directed toward oneself and others—and hence moral activity.

It is these members of society which make it both possible—as they provide it with reliable sources of human capital—and worthwhile (for both the individual and collective), for they enrich it utilely in every imaginable hedonic sense: intellectually, socially, financially, culturally, etc. In doing so, they benefit both the whole and its parts, as represented by individual citizens, and hence fulfill the promise of society's original and maximal potential. Their self-reliance is essential in their classification because it minimizes their utile input and maximizes their output.

So, who specifically are the New Aristocrats? They are not (necessarily) the kings and queens, but the philosophers and poets, the artists, the opera singers and composers, the makers of exquisite sculpture, the master cabinetmaker, the biochemist curing cancer to the civil engineer optimizing traffic patterns in a busy metropolis, the trial lawyer participating in the necessary tradition of jurisprudence, the professor, the beloved comedian. And then there is the baker and butcher, janitor and construction worker, tree surgeon and rugby star, the sexologist and personal trainer, the subway driver, the flight attendant, the rubbish collector. The common theme between them is not glamour or intelligence, fame or fortune, but rather usefulness. An inextinguishable capacity, existent by mere virtue of simply being human and able, for contributing and bettering society. Every man is born an aristocrat. His choices determine whether he lives and dies as one. This inclusivity is the true magic of the New Aristocracy. It is a social class not defined by its relation to others—an external source of identity—but rather its self-contained assessment of worth. Cumulatively, they produce a 'cultural bourgeoisie' which safeguards within society not only its material prosperity, but so too its moral and aesthetic culture through their commitment to diverse utile output, made most efficient by pursuit of self-interests, rather than wholly altruistic and often self-defeating impulses, which collectively leads to diversification of labor and maximal collective benefit.

The New Aristocrats are the self-reliant, the useful, the contributors, the law-abiding (whenever the law is coincident with objective morality, and the disobedient when it is not), the engines of utility. Those industrious, producing men who make morality possible, and practice its craft. Their affiliation is not based on race or social class, but personal merit, the result of self-willed actions and the moral intentions behind them. NAs are providers and consumers of the *widest* (farthest-affecting populationally) and *highest* (quality) utility. They are, in short, the producers of beauty, itself best defined as pure utility experienced without contrary sensation. They are those who make life worth living, those who contribute not simply for themselves—the Equiist-mandated moral minimum—but for the good of the collective in a premium manner. So long as these conditions are met, those in question are New Aristocrats. However, often concurrent with these characteristics, the truest NAs experience the highest utile resources for themselves, agents equal in moral consideration to those affected by their actions. They understand the importance of the good life defined as much in its moral obligations as in the niceties of refined living—from the fine arts to the reading of classics to the value of fashion. These are things to be pursued not because of their criticality, but rather because their marginal utility permits the elevation of a lifestyle from the enjoyed to the savored. To attain true aristocratic status however, these refinements cannot be the bulk of one's specialization, rather than the necessity of good and important works whose benefit is profound for the widest number, in the most impactful manner. If this is achievable, and directed toward those whose capacity for utile production is less than one's own, and whereby one's own happiness, desert and the efficiency of utility output is, per expensive tastes, increased by the pursuit of refinements, then in such a case an aristocrat may permissibly prioritize his own enjoyment, since failure to do so could decrease his utility and subsequent capacity for enjoying the appropriate mental attitude and willingness to maximally contribute toward the more pressing utility dues of deserving others.

The aristocrat is the human ideal—a type of excellence inextricable from the good life of its possessor and whose opportunity may be experienced by those his actions affect. It is this good life—one which selects the highest-quality utile sources in all spheres of endeavor, from the intellectual to the athletic—

which typifies the utmost potential of our hedonic flourishing. While it ought to be the goal of every man to become a New Aristocrat, far more fail inclusion into this ultimate gentlemen's club not because of intrinsic limitations so much as lacked effort. Obedience to the UML and the tenets of MU are in short what promote *eudaimonia*, for it ultimately provides the prerequisite knowledge of our moral desert by providing our talents and efforts for the highest and widest pleasures of others (when, as often they would, such interests supersede our own—themselves only a priority when more efficiently aligned with the UML), and in doing so by the rules of equity in the UML, granting ourselves the desert of pleasure gleaned from interpersonal exchanges.

One criticism of my philosophy shall no doubt be the alleged 'disproportionate' amount of lucre accessible by the ruling New Aristocracy. That such elitism shall indubitably result in corruption, in alienation of duty and bear antipathy toward the under-classes. This proves false on two counts; there is not any ecopolitical conception or historical variant without which a ruling class is necessary, and/or one in which it does not possess 'disproportionate' access to resources. Unlike in past systems however, the New Aristocracy's greater share of entitlement is not the result of arbitrary status or historical inertia, but personal merit. Secondly, by virtue of their merit being based upon utility output, isolation from the masses is unlikely since it is only their superior productivity which distinguishes them from lesser producers. Moreover, their number shall always remain so small, whatever greater proportion of resources they possess shall both be negligible relative to total societal resources (and hence not socially destabilizing), and put to the most efficient use for the regeneration of highest pleasures relative to any other class.

Ecopolitically, the New Aristocrats are productive, contributing members of society who view the government as a sentinel whose principal objective is to serve and protect, but not to provide beyond the provisions of *fundamental* equality of opportunity (as a greater standard has been evinced by history to degenerate into economic unviability and anti-libertarian intrusiveness). They represent the moral, personal and practical goal of all individuals, and the lifeblood behind any society superior to an anarchistic syndicate or state of nature, or similarly any one which blindly values its lowest-producing members for no reason other than the fact of their formal citizenship. It recognizes the importance of productivity as the highest individual and collective good, and, upon recognizing the eternal inequality of individuals (except before the law—a utile rule), that government intervention shall never cure social and economic ills as efficiently as personal motivation. This limitation on the part of the State arises, most succinctly, as a result of its lacked monopoly of information regarding the personal wants and incentives of individuals which most closely align with their original talents and desires which, when freely permitted to be acted upon, optimize both personal and collective utility. That is, no dirigisme may be so perfect as to trump the efficiency of the free marketplace of economic, informational and labor exchange. Such motivation is otherwise stunted in the presence of half-hearted economic measures which shall always fall short of the productivity invigorated by self-reliance, for they result in the masses settling usually for less than their materialistic and ecopolitical optimal potential in the place of tranquilizingly addictive and comfortable government handouts. The seductive ease of such provisions recalls a chilling prophecy of that most feared government which destroys itself and its people once willing to bribe them with their own money. The same is true here; people who succumb to the ease of relying on the government for sustentation therefore settle for reduced utility and are themselves incentivized to produce less, owing to the transactional costs of its delivery to them through the bureaucratic monolith that is ever the State. Alternatively, their individual pursuit of preference satisfaction via the market shall always result in higher utility returns, owing to the proximal efficiencies of the market and there existing fewer middlemen. The cost for this superior utility provision (to the producer), which shall yield greater utility production (to others), owing to its being expended more directly to its recipients (who, in turn, may more efficiently compensate it), is of course, greater effort than the mediocrity of accepting the government's half-way measures. The absence of such measures, of course, may increase societal inequality, but this is untroubling when we consider that this is the natural condition, and that attempts by the State to pervert this reality shall only result in unsustainable and suboptimal utility output on the part of society, most harshly neglecting its highest-contributing individuals, who, by virtue of their relative importance, have a greater stake in resource access. Those who would argue that it is only the government which prevents the socio-structural inequalities which would otherwise result from the market would be well-advised to note that oftentimes government programs continue to reflect and further solidify such inequities by sanctioning them. Only in the absence of such State-provided misguided charity does exist the amplest motivation in one becoming a maximally-efficient utility engine, for himself and therefore others. Just as there is no safety net, there is no ceiling on opportunity necessitated by a broadly non-distributive economy. Only when one is confident in the freedom to fail, is he best encouraged to fulfill his utmost potential. The government should encourage this type of lean and efficient ecopolitical environment, for it maximizes the liberty and economic freedom of its citizens, promoting both individual and collective utility output, personal responsibility, research and innovation. Only when such self-reliance produces exceptional individuals so successful and abusive of their positions that fair competition is hampered, may the government legitimately interfere; premature interference in these matters is the deceptive handsel of the paternalistic government which ultimately corrupts itself and its society on the premise of its own twisted idealism. The clearest method to prevent this cataclysm is the sustained paucity of governmental power and institutions. The crux of the matter, no doubt, is to ensure the idoneous balance of power so that governments may curtail unfair ecopolitical practices yet not be tempted by virtue of this specific monopoly of power to be inclined toward its expansion in other spheres, of which, once this trend commences, history reveals is virtually irreversible short of revolution—traditionally the most tumultuous and disastrous of social and ecopolitical events. In short, the State ought not restrict opportunities, but provide only the freedom for their incubation. Where there is doubt regarding intervention toward reducing inequality at the risk of tyranny, the former is always preferable, for it is reversible through the same channels of market enterprise which bore it, whereas the latter is not subject to rectification absent violent upheaval.

But what of the New Aristocrats' due power? Just as the aristocrats' power of ancient Greece was legitimized owing to their moral or intellectual supremacy (at least originally as was conceived, prior to the custom of inherited titles), so too must we return to this initial understanding of meritocracy. Thus, the NA domain is that of 'rule of the best' in all matters of human endeavor—from economic to political. NAs exist in all fields, and represent the elites within each, whereby both specialized talent and ardor typify their uniform character. In two of the most prominent areas, economics and politics, NAs rule in practice—and ought do so normatively—for distinct reasons. Politically, NAs represent not necessarily elected representatives, but those career bureaucrats whose specialized knowledge comes about through extensive training and devotion to particular fields. Just as one would not entrust the education of his child to a layman unfamiliar with educational science, so too must we not freely assume that political knowledge is uniquely accessible to the untrained majority. In fact, owing to the extremely sensitive and far-reaching import of the political, its treatment must be dealt with especially; short of matters of significant to extreme interest on the part of the majority, whereby their input is either advantageous or necessary toward social change, the crafting of both domestic and foreign policy should fall within the purview of governmental elites, owing to each discipline's requisite training and stability, the latter best secured institutionally rather than per the vagaries of the public whim.

Politics, therefore, is not an especial discipline regarding the importance and existence of expertise; just as the stonemason must toil at his craft, so too must the diplomat and bureaucrat. Politics may be a spectator sport, but it is one best played by professionals. The inevitable fear which arises in response to advocacies for this form of elite-driven government is often populist in sentiment and deeply naïve in reality. The most familiar argument brought against such elitism is the prophecy that elites will soon become corrupted by their power and irreversibly alienated from a now-helpless populace. This is historically unsubstantiated, unlike the investiture of power into the hands of a single man likelier destined to become tyrannical, and disregards the fact that a bureaucratic class may always be successfully threatened by what must remain an independent military and judiciary and the numerical superiority of the public.

Not only do all governments function stably per the rule of elites, but it is in the public interest that they do. Just as a leader cannot lead if equal to his followers, a government cannot be led except by those superior to their masses. This is not a deliberately harsh observation, but an inescapable truth. Only when a bureaucratic class behaves sustainably detrimental or singularly egregious to the populace shall the latter suitably rise up; in such periods of renewal, political change is inevitable. When it is absent, the public reveals it deserves the fruits of its inaction. The ideal society requires no heroes to function well, but when it does not, and no heroes are to be found, every man deserves the fate of injurious governance.

Democratic participation is not a right, but a privilege, for to interfere in matters of State and directly affect the lives of others is a power entitled only to those with a demonstrated respect for the welfare of their fellow man. Why do so many unreflectively consider political participation a right? One would not entrust a layman with the care of his sickly relative, or a novice with the construction of a bridge. Why then permit the unenlightened a stake in the gravest affair of all—the administration of a body politic, and hence, the oversight of those social conditions which make civilized existence possible? Freedom without security is anarchy; order without freedom is despotism. Both doomed scenarios are averted in our framework, because within the hands of the elite. Similarly, freedom does not entail the right to behave unreasonably, and hence intentionally promote pain or engage in immoral behavior. This is because freedom is not a right but a privilege based upon its necessary usage as a means of maximizing utility, its only worthy function. In this regard it is an intermediary toward a desired end, and so long as this end may not be predictably achieved, freedom should not be granted.

Economically, NAs represent another brand of elite, this time in terms of wealth—a metric which, when properly assigned, corresponds to individual net utility output, the value of which is determinable through firstly its quality and secondly, quantity (and valuated through the free market), again subscribing to the UML. Often, it includes the third aspect of extending utile opportunities to others, often in the form of available employment. For many, such a conception of economic desert is intuitive; for others it is unabashedly boorish and a defense of the *status quo*. For those Rawlsians amongst us, such an arrangement is inherently discriminatory owing to the existence of a natural aristocracy—whereby unequal genetic, physical and familial circumstances create an unlevel playing field in life. The existence of such an unfortunate reality is not to be denied, but rather somberly dealt with. As shortly to be furthered, justice is a matter of what is both humanly actionable *and* prescriptive on the basis of equity. While issues such as natural inequalities are pre-humanly actionable, economic redistribution on the basis of variances in talent is, while possible, *not* prescriptive. It violates the equity of actions, requiring significant intrusions on the part of the State which would almost instantly and inevitably result in economic inefficiencies (the result of luck and disparities in financial talents) and ultimately catastrophic class warfare initiated by resentful elites, whose victory would be assured owing to their disproportionate strength in real terms (*i.e.*, societal utile output). It is thus practical and normative that goods be distributed per utility output rather than necessarily contrived and more counterintuitive schemes. Lastly, one is also advised to recall an argument advanced by Nozick regarding the moral desert of elites who, despite their initial natural talent, must also labor to cultivate it—a process which itself augments worthiness of the fruits of such talent.

In closing, the New Aristocracy is a conception of class based upon superior merit, where said merit is the result not only of greater quantitative utile output, but more importantly, its superior quality. This is not to dismiss the prior necessity of lower-quality goods such as food in place of opera, but that, *ceteris paribus*, and in the absence of existential threats or those conditions which make existence unreasonably and unnecessarily lessened in quality, merit—or utile desert—is firstly a function of the quality of one's output, followed by quantity. In so doing, whereas tangible utility output is the first criterion of moral desert, social refinement and the sophistication of one's lifestyle becomes a secondary, though distinct, source of moral worthiness. This is because the *way* one lives is a determinant of the quality of pleasure extractable by said agent; a patron or consumer of the arts, for instance, is liable to savor a richer life than one interested in mass pop culture. While spreading higher pleasures to the greatest number possible is the most significant moral goal, one's lifestyle enters the equation insofar as it beneficially or deleteriously affects at least one individual—our agent in question. Thus, while of secondary priority, it does affect at least one agent, and lesser so those who relate with him; this is the primary framework upon which high culture and socially-cohesive traditions are diffused and valued throughout society.

What does this dual conception of tangible productivity and lifestyle choice signal? It permits an innovative amalgamation of personal industry and desert twinned with a social class structure, fusing together notions of classical liberalism with traditional conservatism. The latter is formed by an association underpinned by commonly agreed upon *individual hedonic tastes*— that is, atomistic socioeconomic compatibility rather than organic class-wide solidarity. Accordingly, notions such as *noblesse oblige* become largely antiquated, for classes are not monolithic entities, but the rational organization of individuals sharing mutual utile capacities and inclinations. Duty as the offspring of privilege becomes an individual, not collective, charge. Much as their interests are normally prioritized because of their relative greater importance in the vital utile provisions within society, the interests of lower utile classes are brought to the fore when their sustainable productivity is threatened unless proper resource distribution occurs. Accordingly, this view of the New Aristocracy does not present it as a disembodied ruling class, but rather places it firmly within a just depiction of a society in which each class is indispensable, but where the relative worth of members within each class varies based upon the scarcity of their relative utile output capacity. So long as each class respects its boundaries—that is, expects no more than its just due commensurate with utile output—society shall remain stable and beneficial to all class members. Class stratification is inevitable owing to the disparate utile demands required of individual citizens, and accordingly, the relative value of their production separates those classes based upon the numbers capable of their creation. Varying utile output capacities are inevitable, yet what is in the reasonable self-interest of each individual class is also in the holistic interest of society overall.

What is Justice?

As we have briefly discussed, the issue of justice exists only so far as man has the capacity for action; that is, matters involving pre-human intervention are devoid of any characteristics of justice or injustice, as the latter is absent agency or moral intent, qualities required in the determination of just conduct. Thus, only what involves intentional action may be classified as just or unjust, and of that realm, it too must be prescriptive. In short, *justice is hedonic reciprocity*, a balancing of utile resources established via the equality of two or more actors' intentions and the magnitude of the impact of their actions, whether positively or negatively utile. Accordingly, justice is a median upon a hedonic continuum reflective of interpersonal behavior, the two extremes being mercy (extreme, undue, benevolence) and cruelty (extreme, undue punishment). It is the stasis reflective of moral equilibrium. Those concerned with its enforcement should not conflate its existence therefore, as is often done, with the processes of forgiveness when it is unreasonable to forgive a particular infraction, just as it ought not always necessitate revenge—a wholly permissible practice—if a given action was the result of unforseeable ambsace or reasonable, and hence pardonable, imperfection on the part of the agent.

What are the implications of this view of justice? They are multitudinous and diverse. First we shall discuss normativity before examining the qualitative shifts occurring in our performance of justice, dependent upon the populational context being used. Justice is a moral baseline; that is, all action which does not at least exist justly, is immoral and by itself, unacceptable. This is not to say, of course, that a man may not ever behave unjustly in his life and not be pardoned, for the very concept of acceptance of imperfection—captured in the benevolence aspect in the UML which pardons negligible shortcomings—is, while incompatible with justice proper, nonetheless caught within the purview of forgiveness, that is to say, benevolence. However, looking at things purely theoretically, it is possible to envisage a man who is, per the Bard's recommendation, neither a borrower nor a lender be, one who exists perfectly equitably with his peers. This man is moral, though minimally so; the reason being that he has adequately labored in exchanges for the costly utile resources he has needed to consume, a necessary toil owing to the agent-neutrality mandated by any moral theory based upon reason, whose proper application shall inevitably inform one of the necessity of both sympathizing and perhaps empathizing equally with the experiences of other agents, *provided of course their interests are non-competitive, and whereby competition, if existent, requires a moral hierarchy to be assigned owing to the impossibility of satisfying all interests in certain cases, the result of either opposing wills or limited resources.* Sympathy is the prerequisite of moral behavior, itself important because it is independent of perspective.

Justice is the baseline of moral obligation because it necessitates one pays sufficiently for the pleasures he receives in life, of which has already been shown are always costly. To do less than this is to be a utility vacuum, to be more is desirable for the inherent good that is hedonic maximization but unnecessary because one is now no longer being duly compensated for his labors; his have become acts of charity. Returning to an earlier point regarding the issue of competing interests, because there are certain instances in which universal justice is unachievable, the UML captures the greatest possible sense of justice, by virtue of ensuring the highest quality dues are established first. Even a man who is not perfectly just in his life, and in fact not benevolent at all, though not cruel, is likely morally acceptable, for others ought, by virtue of their recommended benevolence, pardon his minor shortfalls, though nevertheless recognize his moral rights to resources nothing beyond the most minimally superior to the reprobate, and subsequent to all holistically just and benevolent agents, whose *net* utile production exceeds his own.

Let us now turn to how justice applies to disparate populational spheres. On the intrapersonal level, such requires some explanation. Because justice involves an actionable discourse between two or more agents, intrapersonal justice is an incoherent concept; it does not exist. Rather, all action self-directed may be viewed as benevolent, as it involves the unilateral distribution of utile resources to oneself for personal enjoyment. Interpersonally, justice becomes a matter of balance between two or more agents' actions and intents. While intent is critical in the determination of justice, it is nevertheless the far more difficult to assess, and consequently, in matters of practically determining equity, we must often look to the magnitude of one's actions in determining their due response. Because justice is a function of agency and hence of the human realm, issues of rectifying historical or natural inequalities are *not* issues of justice, but of benevolence, as the aforesaid conditions invoke instances of pre-actionability on the part of those moral agents involved. This takes us into examining extrapersonal and macroscopic justice, whereby ecopolitical arguments in favor of schemes ranging from redistributive economies so as to uplift the inter-generationally impoverished to returning historically coercive land acquisitions to their original owners are all beyond the sphere of justice and instead exist as matters of benevolence, which, though themselves intrinsically desirable by virtue of their provision of the inherent good that is pleasure, are nevertheless optional on the part of members of society to undertake.

Continuing our discussions of the ecopolitical ramifications of justice include the involuntarily non-autonomous. For these INAs—those without full cognitive or physical capacity, often the result of extremes of age (whether developing children or the aged)—justice becomes a matter of charity, though one which is acutely important and desirable. For example, the decision to raise a child entails certain obligations upon the parent owing to the foreseeability of his actions, whereby he is obligated to bring up the child to that point developmentally where he is self-sufficient. This specific case is intimately entwined with justice, because the parent's decision to have the child creates a dependency upon the latter, of which, if not appropriately treated, results in the harm of that child, thereby creating an unjust situation. The elderly pose a slightly more complex problem, insofar as they are no longer directly dependent upon others, and the bulk of their utility has been produced and returned back to them via income and other social goods made possible through fair economic exchanges. Whereas they are still requiring of utile goods, their provision becomes a matter of charity, which, however morally desirable owing to our capacity for intellectualizing its preferability—a lynchpin of the soundness of virtually any moral sense—is beyond the scope of strict justice.

Moreover, what to do with criminality? Criminal behavior constitutes one of the most important spheres of applied justice, and is one woefully misunderstood in contemporary society by scholars and laymen alike. Justice is, as mentioned, a matter of hedonic reciprocity, accordant with the intent and magnitude of one's actions. Subsequently, malicious behavior should not only be punished with an equal magnitude to those it victimizes, but an additional punishment which corresponds to the initial malicious intent required to harm an unsuspecting and undeserving other which upset the former *status quo* of neither agent being harmed or aided by either. While it may be difficult to initially understand the logic of this position, consider it in reverse: agent X, of sound mind, intentionally steals $100 from agent Y, a lawabiding citizen totally undeserving of such harmful treatment. Almost all would cursorily agree that the most just solution to this unjust scenario would be the requisition of $100 by Y from X. But, is this truly fair? For, Y incurred not only the loss of his wealth, but the aggravation and stress associated with his due rights and property having been infringed. Such undercuts an important expectation of safety necessary in the continued functioning of society; those responsible for the fear such a threatened expectation causes must be punished not just for their principal harm, but also the generation of unexpected apprehension as well insofar as they remove from another a vital sense of security resultant from the belief that others shall respect their rights, and vice versa. Y was cheated despite having followed the rules, and to provide X with his same identical misfortune is to disregard the premeditation on X's part which unilaterally resulted in this situation. It would be unfair for each agent to be deprived equally in this scenario, for only X was responsible for its initiation, and ought to be subsequently punished further for his voluntary commission of this imbalance of a formerly stable *status quo*. Essentially, his extra punishment should not be the result of his intent to commit the crime (for only actions, not intentions, should receive any due), but because the perpetrator is always less morally deserving than the innocent, and in the final analysis, if justice is to be done, must be punished more severely—a logic which holds in all acts of revenge. It is not herein imagined for a moment that this additive punishment is easily calculable, nor that it does not have distinct boundaries, but it is necessary for the true establishment of justice between persons.

Equiism adopts a retributive-rehabilitationist theory of punishment, whereby the first priority of just sentencing is the prioritization of victims' suffering, assuming that since the offender has already acted wrongfully, his punishment must precede rehabilitation, for if not, then he benefits from his crimes, relative to those afflicted with his harmful actions. As for rehabilitation, it ought come only subsequent to punishment, and extend only so far as the promotion of utility among other members of society and the offender in question subsequent to the end of his sentence. The extensive institutionalization of rehabilitation is to be treated with skepticism owing to the inefficacy of bureaucratic capacities for personality modification, as opposed to self-willed initiative on the part of the malefactor. Moreover, the issue of economic justice enters into the equation of rehabilitation; unless it can be specifically shown that such programs significantly deter recidivism per given crimes, to mandate that law-abiding citizens pay for the improvement of those who violate their rights is preposterous and unjust to them. Lastly, deterrence theory is opposed by Equiist thought because it violates understandings of justice on two theoretical counts, let alone its dubious efficacy in practice: 1) it *preemptively* attempts to quell crime, thereby adopting a misguided view of intentionality which can only be judged and sentenced subsequent to its enactment and proportionate to the specifics of its situational context, rather than its standardized treatment (for otherwise it views as guilty those who have yet to act criminally, likely doing so disproportionately as well), and 2) it adopts an excessive manner of punishment to make plausible its preemptive threat upon as-yet unfulfilled (if even existent) criminal intentions.

In closing, justice is of vital importance in morality because it requires us to take hedonic responsibility for our actions—

that is, that we may be rewarded with pleasure for the moral, and punished with pain for the iniquitous. Receipt of singularly undeserved pleasures, but ones which are entitled to us so long as we exhibit moral fundamentality, and so long as their receipt does not exploit the efforts unreturned but equitably rewarded to another, does not violate justice, but such free pleasures are rare and often the result of luck independent from human contrivance (*e.g.*, one finds a raw diamond in an unexplored cave and sells it for huge profit). Moreover, while we need only behave justly toward others, we must too be charitable if ourselves partaking in its fruits, for otherwise, we become exploitative and unjust—of which must be avoided to preserve moral fundamentality—in the process.

Justice in Punishment

The purpose of justice is to exact a balance of utility, as determined by intent and measured by the magnitude of action. Thus, just as cruelty is an example of deficient equity, so too is mercy an example of extreme morality in the form of charity. While the latter is oftentimes praiseworthy and distinctly good, sometimes it constitutes a perversion of justice and a disregard of genuine desert. Therefore, acts must be judged on their intent, and treated per their consequential magnitude. While extenuating circumstances may either constitute calls for harshness or leniency in human dealings, the majority shall likely require balance. This entails that no response to any act, however heinous, is unthinkable, and that capital punishment is clearly a viable option. Extending this further, the humaneness of much capital punishment itself appears incommensurate with the brutality of the crimes which often mandate its implementation; not only would reciprocal crimes have to be directed toward the offenders in order to achieve balance, but also a slightly greater punishment so as to punish them for their evil disruption of the *status quo ante*, ensuring that their suffering exceeds that of their undeserving victims. In this sense, punishment is not meant to be directed at ill will or malicious intent per se, but rather to ensure that the relative harms done are balanced commensurate with the roles of each actor. It is unfair for a senselessly shot innocent pedestrian to receive the same punishment as his murderers (who, let us say, are also shot and killed by firing squad), not because the latter should be punished for their intent to kill, but because their unsolicited and initial violation of a *status quo* respect for rights must be penalized so as to ensure that the consequences of punishment are commensurate to the actions of agents (and to signal to other would-be offenders that their punishment shall be sufficiently harsher than the misfortune of their victims). Thus, punishment must fit the crime; therefore, where malicious intent is present (for otherwise, when absent, a crime is but an accident or negligence, itself deserving of reprimand though considerably less than malice), justice in punishment necessitates that the consequences of actions reflect their relative impacts on each actor, as determined by each agent's unique responsibility for a given impact upon those others with whom he interacted.

For the sake of institutional and widespread stability, the courts should be the arbiters of matters of justice, but it is not morally impermissible to personally seek revenge, and vigilantism is justified, for one need not a personal stake to pursue justice, but is, within reason, obligated to this end by virtue of rationally understanding it as a good (this objective understanding being the same type of impartial basis that moral action's desirability is based upon). Nevertheless, this appears to violate the oft-overriding utile rule against vigilantism, for rather than guaranteeing impartial justice, self-delusion and misguidance may likely threaten its course.

Injustice must not be tolerated, and swiftly punished. Incarceration and community-improvement sentences must serve the dual function of denying offenders' ample access to utility, whilst simultaneously converting them into utility engines, thereby making them useful whereas their prior deviant behavior was utility-decreasing. Thus, garbage clean-up, light manufacturing and the like are to be advised, simultaneously demonstrating to them the self-improving process of returning to an utility-increasing capacity—a lesson which must be learnt in order for their successful restoration to a future life devoid of crime. This sense of rehabilitation is important, but not so much as their needed punishment, for victims' rights must supersede those who violate them, and consequently, before the latter ought to be improved, such charity cannot come before the justice inherent in their punishment. Rehabilitation ought not to drain significant resources from the polis, for in doing so, the law-abiding are made to pay for the transgressions of the deviant.

PART V: UNIFICATION

PHILOSOPHY IS UNIQUE amongst sciences. Unlike all other disciplines (with the possible exception of art), it does not exhibit manners of consistent, irreversible progress, whereby its history inevitably serves as the foundation for each successive generation of new yet related ideas. Accordingly, the indecision, regression and infighting which characterize this field have become major sources of its benign contempt by those who do not practice this most irresolute craft. Just as reincarnated ideas upstage newer ones only to be later made once again passé, so too does the cyclical aporia of these deadlocks never cease. It is the bastion of the idle intellectual and the dreamy sophomore, a vessel of idealities absent any usefulness which bear the potential for dangerous new ideologies when untempered by the distinct aura of being so many expertly term 'reality.' While I personally cannot lay claim to such an incisive view of just what this reality is, I am apparently in the minority—that is, those few who remain unwilling to *know* a thing simply because its operational definition is reached by an unquestioning consensus. The unremitting efforts made by philosophy to pierce the hoary assumptions in such a definition have made it a perennial target by non-philosophy scholars and laymen alike. Men of such minds should not waste talent in the futile pursuits of measuring utils and burdening college freshmen to locate imaginary chairs, surely?

The criticisms leveled at philosophy as an arcane and inutile field are not altogether unmerited. While the joys of attempting to decipher the Platonic Forms or pinpoint the boundaries of absolute reality may be intellectually rewarding—moral goods in and of themselves—such efforts do little to promote the *public* good. Because philosophy is singularly unique in its versatility in achieving this end, to divert its efforts away from so noble a goal would prove injudicious at best and immorally negligent at worst. One of the chief impediments in facilitating this transition is the lack of consensus among philosophers in significant areas of study, namely ethics and epistemology. Schisms are non-unique to philosophy, but their intensity is; nowhere in the natural or social sciences does such bickering occur from so irreconcilably disparate sides of an issue. For while physicists may disagree about the best course toward unifying quantum mechanics with general relativity, they do not disagree about the existence of atoms or subatomic particles, the four fundamental forces, etc. Meanwhile, ethicists are still debating whether moral propositions are real while epistemologists doubt knowledge of our very existence. For now, let us confine our interest to ethics. For centuries, entirely distinct schools of thought have remained incompatible with one another. I speak of course of the three most important: deontology, consequentialism and virtue ethics. Before it may find greater practical application, philosophy as a whole must first sort itself out internally, and to that end, must become a unified science. Not only is this possible, but in fact has already been achieved in the formulation below.

Let us first begin with the more pronounced rift in moral philosophy—that between deontology and consequentialism. Here, more than with virtue ethics, is the seeming incompatibility between theories most profound. Simply, whereas deontology looks to some intrinsic feature of rules as morally binding, regardless of the consequences their adherence precipitates, consequentialism looks to the intended consequences of an act in determining its moral status. At first glance, and in fact, those had by thinkers for centuries, this apparent dilemma is irresolvable. The solution however, appears in a new understanding of what consequentialism is all about.

To say that a consequentialist looks solely to the consequence of his action as the determinant of its moral status is inaccurate as it implies both that the moral status of an act can only be ascribed following its execution and that intent is meaningless in moral determinations. Both are flawed views. Rather, it is accurate to say a consequentialist looks to the *intended consequence* of his action as the determinant of its moral status. This is sensible because moral worth is a function of intent independent of consequence, provided one attempts to fulfill that intent via non-negligent action. If one were to eradicate intent as a criterion, then morality would become a preposterous game of *ex post facto* value judgments with seriously problematic implications, chief among them that it would necessitate actions as being disconnected from our intentions; in short, moral behavior would not exist conceptually coherent but as the haphazardly retrospective assignment of positive and negative valuations. Such valuations are flawed because they disconnect human agency from the realm of moral action, and more disturbingly, completely prohibit one from consciously engaging in any sense of meaningful ethical behavior. We would lose the free will to act ethically; the merits of our behavior would not only cease to be ours, but would be assigned subsequent to their fruition. Hence, consequentialism must recognize the primacy of intentions, but unlike deontology, appreciate them insofar as they relate to an action's foreseen consequences and *not* its adherence to a particular rule.

In clarifying matters, we now reach the first genuine impasse. Whereas deontology prioritizes what it holds are *inherently moral fixtures* of rules, consequentialism prioritizes *intended consequences*. Because it is undoubtedly the most popular brand of consequentialism, and the one advocated here, we shall hereby understand the prioritized consequences in question to be hedonic in nature; that is, happiness-maximizing. Thus, deontology favors intrinsic moral rules (often, though not necessarily, hedonic in nature), consequentialism those actions whose intended consequences are happiness-maximizing. As just mentioned, deontology usually, though not always, seeks adherence to rules which, implicitly or explicitly, are utility-maximizing. For example, any absolute proscription on murder would certainly be based, at least in part, on the principle that ending a life is intrinsically undesirable *because it reduces or eliminates its capacity for the experience of pleasure*, whereby a deontologist likely assumes pleasure is its own good. Some of the rules advanced however, are not as clear-cut; for instance, the issue of lying. For Kant, the morality of the act had nothing to do with the maximization of pleasure but rather the maintenance of a stable and truthful linguistic framework otherwise threatened by the undermining act of lying (though, one may argue, such irreducibly concerns itself with questions of utility nevertheless, as regards the functional value of a reliable language not distortive of truth external to linguistic constructions). Such an example remains the exception, and is further marginalized by its patent risibility. In reconciling deontology and consequentialism, we shall focus on the former's more popular incarnations as they pertain to other-regarding acts such as proscriptions on murder, torture[1], coercion, harm and any acts which use others as a means to an end contrary to their will.

How do these blend with consequentialism? The answer lies not so much in either theory itself, but rather in their disparate perspectival treatments of the individual, a dichotomy herein termed the *Rational/Experiential Impasse*. Overcoming this particular obstacle has been the most significant hindrance in reconciling these two schools; doing so comes about not as a result of their being reconcilable, but in the examination of the merits of each theory's conception of the individual, and subsequent recognition of how one proves superior to the other in those particular situations in which both conceptions cannot coexist.

Rational/Experiential Impasse

The above-cited issue is the foremost obstruction in the unification of deontology and consequentialism. Specifically, the problem lies in how each views the individual. The underlying rationale of deontological principles views individuals as dis-

---

1 There is no proscription against torture if toward the greater good based solely upon utilitarian calculation, assuming its practices are conducted responsibly and with reasonable assurance of the guilt of the interrogated. The interrogated may be permissibly subjected to such harm because they do not possess an equal moral standing to innocent victims by virtue of their unprovoked aggressions against them.

crete and non-aggregable units of conscious experience. This explains why rules which forbid coercion or using others as means to an end exist; both devalue individual autonomy whose sovereignty is uninfringeable at any cost. Accordingly, deontologists understand individuals to never be permissibly used in pursuit of the collective good if contrary to their will, and some go further in proscribing even voluntary acts of martyrdom as violating the deontological mandate on the preservation of autonomy. Collectively, deontology views individuals from the bottom-up: that is, each of us exists independent of the conscious experience of others, much as our respective utilities cannot be added or subtracted from one another. Because we exist independently, the widest sphere of the moral considerations of the consequences of an action is the individual. Looking at things in the negative sense, this is why deontologists forbid hugely beneficial actions to the greatest number if they may only come about at the harmful cost of even a single innocent individual; many argue that the harm faced by that one individual is not less significant than the benefit received by any one of the many. The benefitted many cannot additively share in each other's pleasure; that is, any one of the benefitted group's utility is not augmented by its being shared by others around him owing to the separation of their respective consciousnesses. Similarly, the harmed innocent cares little about the great benefit he has made possible, for he can only concern himself with the painful reality that is his personal experience. Thus, while maximizing happiness for the greatest number is clearly deontologically praiseworthy, assuming we value pleasure as its own good, to do so at the cost of harming one innocent becomes forbidden because the realm of experience does not extend beyond the individual and cannot be aggregated; consequently, any action which inflicts harm upon even a single individual is qualitatively identical to its infliction upon a thousand. There is no difference *experientially*, since each of the inflicted thousand understands his pain only individually. Altogether, these arguments appeal to the actual and intuitively *experiential* nature of our consciousness, and accordingly constitute the experiential half of the aforementioned impasse.

The other half of our dilemma exists within the realm of consequentialism, and exists as a principally *rational*, and not experiential, phenomenon. This is largely pursuant to the situations with which each school most often handles; utilitarians deal with multiple agents (thereby falling back upon rationality as an objective third-person perspective not favoring any one agent's perspective) unlike deontologists, who look not beyond the individual (thereby not needing to rely on any domain beyond the nature of his experience as their modal logic). Consequentialists, as discussed, look to the intended consequences of their actions for moral valuation. Often, an individual's actions are other-regarding and, since they affect those around him, require that their effects be considered in determining whether such action is morally permissible. For the sake of meaningful argument, we shall discount fringe strands of consequentialism such as egoism (concerned unequally with one's own pleasure) and altruism (concerned unequally with others' pleasure), instead focusing on agent-neutral utilitarianism. Here, we shall examine how utilitarians differ in their moral prioritization of the individual, why this is so, and how, recognizing the two schools are *prima facie* irreconcilable, this debate may be resolved.

Utilitarians do not disregard the importance of the individual, nor can they plausibly discount the discreteness of individual experience. Just as conscious pleasures and pains cannot be additively sensible, so too is it impossible for all individual interests to always be simultaneously satisfiable. And herein lies the crux of the matter: if multiple individual interests, let alone the exercise of their rights, cannot simultaneously always coexist, what to do *then*? Adequately addressing this question shall solve the rational/experiential impasse, and in doing so, it apodictically follows that the answer is not a matter of reconciliation between the two schools, but the demonstration that while the deontological approach is generally sensible, the utilitarian approach subsumes its general applicability, as well as satisfactorily serving the exceptional case, thus proving the superior position. Here is why.

Normally, individual interests, of which we can consider rights to be a special and profound subclass, can coexist with other, different ones, either wholly or with only minor oppositions. A prime example of this might be observed in a queue of customers waiting in a bakery; while everyone wants bread immediately, no one individual can stably pursue his interests without the situation descending into mild anarchy. So, the solution is a negligible sacrifice made of each individual's interest—waiting in line. However, what happens when we up the sacrifice required of competing interests? Let us return to the trolley problem as evidence. Here, we are faced with the choice of killing one, or killing (let us say) five people. We already know omission is not sensible, because it results in a consequence inherently undesirable and deontologically forbidden: the death of innocents. A more accurate phrase would be 'killing of innocents' because such an act of omission would require both intent and subsequent action, of which produces proscribed consequences.

So, why does utilitarianism prove victorious? The answer is because in this special situation of forced choice, whereby all individual rights cannot be respected, only two options exist: their complete disregard (patently ludicrous), or their partial regard. Their partial regard—that is, the saving of some versus none—is preferable because of *rational*, and not experiential, thinking. For a deontologist, the death of one would be the moral equivalent to the death of all, because no one individual can sensibly experience the pleasure of being saved or the pain of being killed to any extent relatable to the other individual(s) in question. Hence, saving one would be experientially equivalent to saving all, and killing one would be experientially equivalent to killing all, since the joy an act of saving would bring, much as the pain the act of killing would bring, would only be experienceable on the individual, single-person level. The reason this perspective is flawed is because it adopts a first-person viewpoint, as opposed to the objective third-person one employed by utilitarianism, necessary because we are dealing with multiple agents (a feature totally disregarded by deontology), none of whom can be reliably said to have an impartial first-person viewpoint. While utilitarianism is capable of recognizing that rights/interests incompatibility may be ameliorated by the satisfaction of the greatest number (assuming all are equally morally worthy), deontology is not, hence failing to adhere to its implicit valuing of certain consequences. Much as the deontologist would be forbidden to kill, he is nevertheless violating this principle *more* by killing five versus one, whereas the utilitarian (ostensibly charged with saving life) is maximizing his adherence to principle by saving the greatest number, for even in the best case scenario a single person must be sacrificed. The alternative, allowing all to die, would be the most egregious betrayal of one's moral duty—whether utilitarian or deontological. This position would hold in any trolley problem variant, whether involving the impersonal dispatching of one via a lever or the forcible pushing of a bystander off the platform—the intent and consequence of each act is the same, only the negligible form different.

Ironically, utilitarianism has long been criticized as a dehumanizing philosophy, that its calculating approach to individuals and their fungibility somehow denies a fundamental humanity not absent in deontological thinking. The opposite proves true, for it is the latter which disregards individual interests when not all can be satisfied, rather allowing that the unfortunate few must necessarily make unfortunate the lot of all others when superior alternatives exist, and utilitarianism that values the individual whenever possible, attempting to maximize his happiness and the number capable of its experience, thereby adopting an impartial, omniscient perspective respectful of all. Utilitarianism, and especially MU, cater to individual tastes, though recognize some are superior to others; when exposed to all, a reasonable individual will recognize the supremacy of some over others (and if not, then he is intellectually inferior—this may appear circular, but it is true nevertheless). Utilitarianism is unique in the fact that it recognizes the inequality of individuals in terms of their characteristics, merit, tastes, behaviors, etc., though is otherwise respectful of their equality as autonomous beings since it is agent-neutral. Self-love is natural and good, but not so compelling as knowledge of the good, itself the prerequisite to happiness because it ensures our sense of moral desert, and hence, pleasure untainted by guilt. Thus, when knowledge of the good compels self-sacrifice toward a greater end, not only does it supersede self-interest, it subsumes it, for any action other than sacrifice in such an instance forfeits our right to happiness, and hence betrays our greatest self-interest of all: the moral worthiness of happiness. Thus, it is firstly our self-love which should make us care about moral duty.

Therefore, utilitarianism in general, and especially MU, is not dehumanizing, but sensitive to the value of each individual life (in terms of its pleasure experienced and capacity for generating pleasure for others), using it as its broadest contextual frame and something only to be sacrificed when a greater value is achievable (a better life, more lives [of greater or lesser quality, the latter requiring an even-larger number], etc.). In fact, its valuing of life per its hedonic quality not only does not dehumanize the individual, but positively paints a heroic conception of one duty-bound toward self-improvement and self-reliance so as not only to be happier for himself, but to become more morally valuable—a motivating mechanism absent from deontic logic since the latter proves indifferent to the *quality* of a life versus its misguidedly unflinching respect for it, independent of its productive capacity or enjoyment (which, when considered, clearly reveals there to exist a hierarchy of lives in terms of their relative value). To be valuable is not a function of our talents, but our highest use of them. Utilitarians do not disregard the importance of the individual, but recognize the objective preferability of satisfying the worthiest interests of some when the interests of all cannot be satisfied. Here, self-reliance is important because it decreases our utile costs for functioning (unlike in those dependent upon others, thus reducing their net utile output), permitting us to exist self-sufficiently, producing maximal utile output—that which exceeds whatever is required for our own sustenance. While it attempts to avoid discussions of sacrifice, it, unlike deontology, can at least cope with them in a far superior manner absent the wider extent of detrimental consequences which would otherwise emerge, the result of deontologists' inability to sacrifice a few for the more. Not only does this latter brand of thinking implicitly undermine deontological principles (since all sound ones must ultimately be based upon utility, as further discussed), but fails to justify them per its fallacious defense of the morality of omission.

It should be noted that the above arguments hold so long as we assume each individual has a morally equal stake in the respect of his interests or rights; that is, that all individuals are of equal merit. If not, then meritocratic utilitarian calculation must step in, as outlined in the UML, whereby numerical concerns are no longer the chief priority so much as the satisfaction/protection of the interests of individuals of higher merit. In such instances, maximization of the highest-quality individuals must surpass even protection of the greatest number (if of lower merit), for the same perspectival reasons as described above. Assuming all interests cannot be satisfied (for if possible, there is no rift between the schools), and individuals vary in merit, then the most meritorious take moral priority. The deontological alternatives, permitting not just a numerical majority of individual interests to be disrespected in deference to a minority, but so too superior individuals of greater merit to be discarded unnecessarily for lesser others, is unthinkably immoral.

Altogether, MU represents, as shown here, a revolutionary theory, in that it advocates a heroic conception of man who is charged to define his own self-worth, and whose worth is practically judged only relative to the moral, and not material, successes of those other men before him. In its treatment of moral values, there is only pleasure. In regard to context, there is only the individual. This brand of individualism which is agent-neutral but individual-focused I refer to as 'hedonic individualism,' for it recognizes that ethical egoism is implied by the above insofar as it is natural (and hence most efficient, rather than contrived altruism) and desirable in our increase of personal happiness to augment our subsequent right to it (*i.e.*, happiness begets the right to protecting and furthering it, since a more joyful existence becomes more morally valuable, and hence of higher priority to protect). Sacrifice is only mandated when issues are significant to preserving one's moral fundamentality, and whereby such required losses are exceeded by the gains made by *worthy others*.

Inherence and Consequence

As already alluded to in the section on omission, another significant area of disagreement between deontology and utilitarianism is the matter of *inherence versus consequence*. That is, deontologists believe there to be fixed and intrinsic moral rules which ought to guide action whereas utilitarians believe the good to be a result of beneficial consequences. The truth lies somewhere in between. As already discussed, the only irrefutable good is plea-sure. To this extent, its maximization is a deontological rule. However, extrahedonic rules, such as absolute prohibitions on killing, bodily harm, theft, misinformation and the like are not in themselves automatically justified, and only so if they intention-ally reduce displeasure. Thus, we find moral consensus between the schools on the matter of the maximization of pleasure, as all coherent deontological rules defend their rationales, directly or indirectly, as a means of achieving some pleasing end.

The divergence however, exists in deontology's understand-ing of there being intrinsic moral rules, made up, in the words of Mackie, as some part of the fabric of the universe. Not only is this intuitively implausible (perhaps moral imperatives lie somewhere between Mars and Jupiter, or the energy levels of an electron), but clearly untestable. Beyond this cursory objec-tion, the idea that moral propositions exist inherently is flawed because what is moral—that is, valued toward achieving some beneficial end—is dependent upon the nature of being. Whereas conquest for a lion is moral owing to its nature and absence of reason, collaboration is preferred amongst humans, even those of superior physicality and capacity for domination. Just as there is no definitive archetype for moral prescription on Earth (the multiplicity of human, animal and plant life is but mere proof if not for the probabilistic likelihood of alien races extraterres-trially), there cannot be any correspondent moral objectivity beyond the realm of our own capacity for self-reflection and as-piration. Of the human realm, no good exists beyond pleasure, and accordingly, it is sensible to build a *human* moral framework upon this value.

Recognizing that pleasure is the only morally-inherent value, and agreed upon by deontologists and consequentialists alike, we may now understand the schism between these schools resulting from squabbles concerning the inherence of extrahe-donic rules. Deontology fallaciously ascribes moral inherence to rules unconnected directly with the increase in pleasure, even though their only argued value can emerge if ultimately con-nected to its augmentation. For example, let us take the classic Kantian proscription on lying: that fibbing ultimately leads to the breakdown of language, is thus exclusively detrimental and ought to be avoided if we assume (as Kant obviously must have) that the loss of language would lead to a decrease in utility, and hence pleasure (likely of a higher, intellectual sort rather than a lower, physicalist one). While it thus might make sense that deontological rules be defended if they ultimately appeal to utility, such is not so considering 1) they are universally binding and 2) fail to take into account competing hedonic priorities. Thus, deontological rules ultimately fail to appeal to their core value of pleasure because they often confuse lesser, derivative values (such as autonomy, truth, etc.) as being of equal or greater priority, thereby decreasing pleasure either in the short- or long-term.

Thus, those rules which do not disregard pleasure as the *only* morally-inherent value, and do so immediately without interposition of Lilliputian and detracting values, are deontologically and consequentially compatible. Beyond this initial compatibility, utilitarian consequence trumps deontological inherence, for the former is concerned only in maximizing the objective good, whereas deontology pursues lower priority mandates which are erroneously understood to be universal and binding, all the while decreasing the efficiency with which the utilitarian mandate—the only and most valid one—ought be pursued.

Deontology as a Special Form of Consequentialism

Indubitably, the case presented for deontological-consequentialist unification is predicated upon the understanding that whereas deontic logic holds generally, in such cases so does utilitarian logic, and that in exceptional cases where the former falls, the latter does not, and ought be taken up. In this schema, we recognize utilitarianism as the subsuming and greater philosophical school, whereby deontology fiddles with derivate rules based upon the simpler and more universalizable premises of its parent. Essentially, owing to pleasure being the only inherent human good, all moral issues must ultimately collapse into discussions of utility.

Clearing up this matter is the first real step toward the unification of ethics. Deontology is a special form of utilitarianism, and a subset of consequentialism. It deals with the general, consequentialism with the specific. Broadly speaking, deontic logic, like rights themselves, is a form of generic rule utilitarianism, its edicts being no more than utile guidelines which generally ought be followed, not only because of their actual utility yield but also because they engender utility-maximizing patterns of behavior more likely to be cultivated than if acts were directed on a case-by-case basis devoid of some overarching protocol. This form of prudent generalization works best with monolithic or large bureaucratic entities, slow and inept, whilst operating at minute levels. For example, while it is *res ipsa loquitur* that an intelligent and politically informed thirteen-year-old ought to be permitted to vote, establishing a generalized higher voting age is sensible considering the rarity of such a case. Understanding deontological rules is similar to understanding the lowest-common-denominator strategy implemented in the formulation of law. Thus, we may understand that filching is not intrinsically immoral, but generally inutile, considering it involves the coercive loss of another's property, whose allocation is generally the most efficient reward of the merit of individuals in society. However, in times of genuine and deserved need, and whereby the theft in question would aid oneself far greater than the victim, it appears not only permissible to engage in such an activity, but morally obligatory. Consider a starving man who comes upon an empty house in the woods with a pantry stocked full of food as a prime example.

We have made an important leap in our clarification of ethics. We have learnt that deontic logic concerns itself with the formulation of general moral guidelines, and that in this capacity, it is a refined extension of utilitarian consequentialism, for all deontic logic, somehow predicated upon the idea of its being beneficial, must ultimately be based upon production of utility. In special circumstances when its blunt mandates ought not or cannot be met, the finer point of utilitarian calculation must be applied case-specifically, thereby stripping our moral philosophy down to its most fundamental first principles. Through and through however, from the general to the specific, we recognize that utility is the binding factor, and that its calculations may occur either through the deontological prism of generality, or the consequentialist one of case-specific analysis. Therefore, we may confidently assert, the right and the good are one and the same.

Virtue Ethics

A cynosure which has scarcely shone in the history of philosophy is now upon us as we near the end of our first tunnel. Deontology and consequentialism (and specifically, MU) have been shown to be two sides of the same coin, hence uniting what had formerly stood as two long and embittered rivals. Such academic acrimony aside, there is still a third major school with which to unite our two newfound brothers. The estrangement of this third school is of a far different nature from that of the previous two, for its divergence exists not so much in its pedantry but in its metaphysical conception of the ethical individual. Whereas both deontology and consequentialism treat the individual as a moral automaton whose mechanical adherence to preconceived rules is the measure of his character, virtue ethics casts a far more human and holistic understanding of the individual as just that—one whose ethicality is determined by the general characteristics of which he is imbued, and not the inflexible duties to which he perfunctorily must adhere. Accordingly, this Aristotelian artifact remains strongly inherited in the minds of most laymen, and is perhaps the most intuitive of all moral theories, judging a man's worth per his holistic nature and its cultivation of a few prized traits. Clearly, this theory seems most sensible if only because it is most aligned with the nature of man, and hence most apt in his appropriate judgment.

However, virtue ethics is not largely passé without good reason; the merit of any good philosophy comes about not solely in its emotional appeal (such as with virtue ethics), but in its rigor when subjected to the further epistemic tests of rational/intuitive exploration and experiential experimentation. To that end, we find the more rule-based tenets of deontology and the singular act-based tenets of consequentialism appealing considering our second requirement of rational exploration, for each supplies an impartial objectivity absent from virtue ethics owing to the moral universality of their mandates, whereas virtue ethics calls for the general appraisal of a man, flaws and all—so nebulous and all-inclusive a scale of judgment that it can all too often prove impossibly difficult to implement, unlike the more exacting former two schools. But what about empirical experience—that is, the real world? Does virtue ethics or its offspring prove superior in this category? I find the answer, perhaps unsatisfactorily, to be blurred; whereas virtue ethics appeals to our Gestaltian sense of the inadequacy of judging a moral agent solely through the additive moral calculation of his individual actions, it fails to supply us the necessary clarity of direction required of many significant and otherwise ambiguous moral decisions in life, ranging from which profession we ought pursue considering our talents to whether we should neglect informing our best friend of his adulterous spouse to how we should spend our disposable income. As far as the practical, experiential value of each school is concerned, it appears a combination, incapable of perfect explication or reduction, of all three is necessary for ideal decisions.

So, we clearly see that virtue ethics has its own distinct place as an emotionally-attractive and partly experience-driven theory. But, how can it fit within our broader understandings of a universal moral theory, and specifically meritocratic utilitarianism and its subsequent UML? The answer is simple in formulation, though slightly more arduous in practice if only because it requires shifting modes of judgment, from the deontological to the consequentialist to the aretaic, dependent upon the circumstance. The common link is not so much their similar patterns of decision-making, but rather the justification for their ultimate implementation. And, what is that common link? Utility. Virtue ethics may best be understood as a unifying piece to the puzzle of a grand theory of ethics insofar as it is a form of rule utilitarianism, but on a far broader and less impersonal scale. Just as rule utilitarianism stresses the importance of the utility of *generalizable rules* (whose discriminate, situation-specific disobedience might prove unsustainable or ultimately inutile owing to transactional costs, slippery slopes, etc.), so too does virtue ethics understand moral behavior as contingent upon the *generalizable characteristics* of men. A man cannot be motivated to consistently act generously because he has intellectualized such behaviors to be intrinsically moral or undergone painstaking Benthamite felicific calculations and is subsequently sufficiently motivated, but rather he acts in such a manner because it is a part of his character—a feature of behavior which brings him comfort when enacted automatically. It is the cultivation of these necessarily-inculcated traits, the result of repetitive education, the imbuements of law and social norms, which make men instinctively desire such behaviors as a heuristic description of some vital portion of their character, thereby being intrinsically motivated to do the right as opposed to being mechanically or computationally inclined. One cannot be held morally responsible unless educated not in what is right and wrong, but how to apply reason in arriving at such conclusions. Every man exposed to minimal social intercourse has, sufficiently activated, this capacity of reasoning, and is hence morally responsible for his acts.

The *emotional* desire to obey our character provides a human complexion to obedience of even the most objective moral imperatives, as in the UML, for we are compelled to do good because we *want* to feelingly and in response to a personal identity which is unique in its self-comprehension to us, and not because we mechanically calculate such to be preferable. Consequently, the development of virtue ethics as a pathway which ensures we come to reflexively value those traits which maximize those behaviors which prioritize merit, beauty, duty, maximal utile output, etc., is the surest means of incorporating them within our broader ethical framework, whereby it transforms into a special form of rule utilitarianism—much as deontology does—but doing so on the level of our personality itself. We thus find that the third and final major school of ethics has become unified upon the common basis of utility.

PART VI: AESTHETICS

What is Art?

IN THE HISTORY OF AESTHETICS, this central question has resulted in so disparate an array of responses that at this point, it almost seems puerile to expect any uncontestable—nigh tractable—discussion of the matter. However, I shall present a theory of art which, despite its inevitable controversy and recent disfavor, has nevertheless stood the test of time as perhaps the most singularly abiding and traditionalist conception we have, by amateurs and aesthetes alike.

Art is the human craft which intentionally acts toward achieving beauty. Beauty is pure pleasure—that is, neither contradicted nor achieved through means contrary to its end form. Art is that which intentionally provides utility in its original form; it is pleasure injected into the conscious experience without diluting intermediaries. Furthermore, it must require presence of mind, for otherwise it is a hedonic accident. Intentionality is required to elevate art into a contrivance with purpose, and hence into the realm of human achievement and valuation; there can be no artistic valuation of that which is haphazard. Of course, beauty absent intent can always be appreciated so long as its end form delivers pure utility. Physical nature is perhaps the starkest example of this exception. While of course the end form is to be savored, it alone cannot qualify as a work of art, for art is not synonymous with beauty; it is a distinctly human achievement, and can only be considered so if requisite of our highest and most human faculties: attention, intention and emotional arousal. A beautiful woman is beauty, but not art.

Equally in the exposition of good art, we may define our subject in terms of what it is not. Much alleged art produces discord in the human spirit—its function is to provoke, condemn and horrify. It is a truism that we learn best from our mistakes, and that the experience of pain is necessary in the adaptation of those mindsets and skills which optimize our capacity for subsequent pleasures. In practice, this is of course true, and art which serves this legitimate function—pursuit of a capacity for higher pleasure and experience—is valid, though nonetheless an inferior aesthetical form for such required compromise on its part. This realm of crudity and reality detracts from the ideal, and thus the unblemished nature of idyllic happiness. No good art can ultimately produce displeasure. Opponents who claim that this idealized conception falsifies the verity of art fail to realize that happiness itself is a principally psychological concept independent of the grittiness of empirical reality, but rather the result of proper attitudinal training of a strong and independent mind. High art corresponds with high discipline in the pursuit of stoically self-reliant happiness.

Formal Realism

Equiism, be it the all-encompassing philosophy that it is, posits a distinct aesthetical theory based heavily upon its ethics, itself based upon the Equiist conception of reason. Formal realism advocates a theory of art as pure utility, appealing to the tripartite epistemic nature of man—that is, the mind, the spirit and the real. The first two are straightforward: intellectual provocation and emotional arousal are key to good art for they heighten its capacity for maximally enriching the areas of pleasure experienced by the consumer. The third characteristic, and first requirement of art—*appeal to reality*—is not a reversion to the crudity just formerly lambasted, but a clarion fidelity to objective reality, the realm in which all our experienceable happiness must dwell. Significant divestiture of the real is ultimately destructive as it falsifies our expectations and creates dependencies for utility within environments beyond our access. In doing so, it deprives us of personal rule over our own sources of happiness, in effect destroying our free will and tranquilizing us into a state of blissful inactivity. Consequently, true art must appeal to objective reality, or reference it through symbols apparent and accurate.

This brings us to our second requirement of art: *conceptual completeness and clarity.* Good art, by its appeal to universal moral features, themselves so defined by their access to utility, must be universal. In doing so, its forms cannot be so abstruse as to be only—and thus dubiously—accessible by a self-proclaimed expert few, but rather all those of suitably refined mind and judgment, the result certainly of personal cultivation, though not pedagogy. Cumulatively, high art born of an appeal to reality and conceptual completeness must usually require a further unofficial characteristic: technical skill, necessary in the rendering of realistic aesthetic creations and detailed simulations.

Formality proves the third requirement, as art's subject matter must be highborn in order to ably deliver the higher forms of pleasure—namely the intellectual, itself divided into the superior provocative challenges of reflection and the secondary petition toward unoriginal and rote scholarly matters. Formal topics in art often involve the sociopolitical and philosophical, deferentially treated neoclassically as a nod to the enduring forms of art itself, in addition to its mere content. In demonstrating formality, art appeals to the innate human sensibilities and character, avoiding the crude and base which constitute our most primitive forms.

Together, these characteristics produce what is the ultimate test of art: the delivery of pure, high utility. However, there remain two additional features of art required in its genuine existence, and independent from its hedonic merit. These are *intentionality* and *originality.* The former is required to separate art from natural beauty and transform it into a firmly human construction. This is important because art is a human activity, and its merit lies in its drawing from, and appealing to, innately human characteristics and abilities. Secondly, this intent must be *original*, thereby requiring that the human imagination and its unique powers for creativity be put to work, thereby relying upon the highest of human ingenuities: intellectual invention in the name of achieving pleasure. If these features are not taken into consideration, then we permit art to include the arbitrary and accidental, the forged and nonhuman. Originality must exist to produce intentionality, because a value of art is its uniqueness as a reflection of the unique capacities of the artist's will; if unoriginal, his intention was not pure and unworthy of admiration. Sunsets and Renoirs blend together as one and the same, no longer separated by the necessary activity of human contrivance and artistic intent, much as a plagiarized Faulkner passage—however pleasing to an unwitting audience—ought misguidedly be viewed aesthetically equivalent to the original. This is unacceptable. Moreover, because of the objective criteria for true art, its merit lies largely independent of the *zeitgeist* in which it was created and any larger, evolutionary historical narrative. Its timeless necessity exists because it appeals to our everlasting need for pure, unfiltered pleasure—a want so rarely sated outside the boundaries of the aesthetic.

The Boundaries of Art

The confines of art extend well beyond the domains of walls and sculpture, blueprint and easel. While painting may be viewed the most classical example of art, additional, and seemingly more exhaustive categories, such as music, literature, architecture and performance—from dance to theatre to film—prove insufficiently inclusive. In fact, any human activity which embodies the above criteria may constitute art. Whether this is culinary science, *haute couture*, aureate oratory or even the pioneering of a new surgical technique—the common denominator is ultimately its capacity for utile production. This is not to say that the function of art is not intermediately instrumental; in fact, quite the opposite is true: it is *directly* instrumental. Whereas much of our behavior seeks to maximize the efficiency of intermediate steps toward the experience of pleasure, art is the most direct approach to its enjoyment, for its sole end is its production. Therefore, art represents the purest and most efficient form of ethical behavior.

High art and low art are respectively divided according to the subtypes of reason to which they appeal. Much as intellectualized art is of the highest variety and the most enduring since a matter of attitude—itself largely independent from external deterioration—the wholly physical and primal represent the basest forms of the aesthetic, and hence, the most fleeting.

The Nature of Taste

If we have defined art, how might we define good taste? Simply, taste is the distinction between art and non-art as made possible via the cultivation of those subtypes of reason whose hedonic demands are satisfied by aesthetic projects. Of course, the cultivation of these subtypes of reason occurs long before they are directed toward the enjoyment of art, and suitably, what appeals to their highest natures, may be suitably classified as art, provided its intentionality, originality and other necessary attributes coexist. Naturally, taste is not something apt for precise delineation, but nonetheless subject to broad characterization. Essentially, it comes about through the exploration of various aesthetic samples, and the application of reason toward the suitable judgment of the merits of each. Therefore, taste is subsequent to the development of reason, a tripartite phenomenon requiring the use of intellect and emotion—both inborn abilities—and experience. Thus, experience comes about as vital in the appreciation of beauty; this does not imply that beauty is relative, but that its keener identification is made possible by the widest examination of the aesthetic.

For the first time, we come to realize that our grand unified theory of ethics extends beyond purely moral boundaries to include aesthetical judgments contingent upon a refined sense of our subtypes of reason being appropriately calibrated to the hierarchy of pleasures. The universality of this theory shall be shown to extend well beyond the realm of axiology, to include politics and other disciplines, becoming in the process, a true theory of everything.

Art as Ethics

Philosophy is an examination of what ought to follow from what is. It is thus, firstly, an examination of truth and then ethics. Art is an ethical activity achieved by the pleasurable revelation of truth. Thus, whereas philosophy dissects truth, art unravels it. It is in that unraveling, when properly done, that the effort required is directed toward sating the highest human potentials: the recognition of truth and moral duty. The process herein described, engages and satisfies our highest capacities for pleasure, and hence, the aesthetic project itself is a moral activity.

Art is the sincerest form of ethics. Because ethics concerns itself with the provision of pleasure, and because art and ethics fall under axiology—the study of value—they both must deal with something man intrinsically prizes. Equiism tells us this indisputable value is pleasure. Art therefore, as in ethics, must be pleasurable, for otherwise it provides nothing to value, and falls short of its mandate. Thus, my conception of art is the generation and representation of 'pure utility'—that is, pleasure uncorrupted and without reliance upon immoral means, ranging from bodily harm to displeasing crudity.

Art is a subset of ethics; ethics is a subset of art. They are inextricably related, though truly, art is most truly a subset of ethics, because ethics is the study of how ought we live and to what end should our actions be directed—art is simply the purest incarnation of that study. Art seeks pleasure in its purest form, whilst ethics informs us of what to value and how to attain it. Thus, ethics precedes art by providing it with a necessary aim (pleasure) and acceptable procedural directives (realism, clarity, formality, etc.). However, art may be purer than applied, rather than theoretical, ethics, for while applied ethics must concern itself with compromise in daily reality and often fundamentality over the likelihood of excellence and certainly over even the possibility of perfection, art need not make such sacrifices, and instead pursue utility in its purest humanly-attainable forms. Because it may be removed from the world, its demands and conflicts, it may be uncontaminated from its flaws. Of course, little thought need be rendered in realizing that ambitious as the aims of art may be, the goal of ethics is more immediate to the human condition, for it stipulates that pleasure not stand alone, but rather be directed into the lives of those most longing and worthy of it.

What, pray tell, of the trepidations of horror films to the draining catharsis of tragedy—why are these aesthetic activities, all seemingly utilely impure, enjoyed? What say us, of a theory of displeasure in art? It is because we do not personally experience these hardships in their fullest form, but observe as a third party, that they become palatable. Moreover, these difficulties are both painful and pleasurable. An intense game of squash is enjoyable, yet simultaneously strenuous. We find pain in exhaustion, though pleasure in physical exertion and mobility. When one topples the other, we continue or cease. These sensations do not exist simultaneously with one another. Sudden death scenes on celluloid frighten, but immediately afterwards our recovery provides us a thrill of excitement and emotional provocation which, once we reestablish is unfounded in reality but only onscreen, we transform into a form of positive energy (or more specifically, the alleviation of displeasure, the functional equivalent of active pleasure)—indicating our ability to intellectually transform the attitudinal reception of emotional arousal from displeasing to pleasing, at least to a certain extent. Tragedy is fascinating because we do not struggle ourselves, but rather observe the travails of others and the human drama which is always thrilling because of its intensity; our voyeurism makes this enjoyable, suggesting life is a struggle in which happiness is the result of superiority in competition. Thus, excitement is intense emotional arousal, predicated upon a natural reaction. In most cases, it is the result of *schadenfreude*—an unfortunate and acutely human trait overcome via the suppression of naturalistic impulse by reason such that we may become a more moral agent and objective aesthetic arbiter.

Similarly, pain conveyed in art is always harmful in itself, unless, for practical reasons unavoidable in the aspiration of a higher plane of consciousness and hedonic comprehension— that is, appreciation of some previously unseen good. While this is normatively untenable, in practice it is occasionally necessary, for perhaps in the sufferings of art we learn to reaffirm our sense of humanity, our capacity for pleasure, our sense of moral purpose—realizations perhaps waning if not forcefully reintroduced by exposure to their contrasting elements. Or, perhaps it is in the exposure to pain that we become more immune to its sharpness, thus maximizing our capacity for longer-held pleasures, now relatively shielded from pains whose effects would otherwise be magnified without such inoculating exposure. Thus, art creative of discord, is only valuable insofar as it must do so in the inescapable and successful attainment of a higher pleasure, and one outweighing the necessary displeasure undergone; that which presents the base to invent repulsion and glorify crudity is, alternatively, tripe, for the true function of art is pursuit of the ideal, of the reasoned—of the happiness-maximizing.

The Contemplation–Comprehension Theory of Jokes

What is a joke? Long ago perhaps thought to be a juvenile if not outright unphilosophical question, for some time it has remained—and persists—a topic of noteworthy and unexpectedly fascinating debate. Before continuing, it is important to note why a section on jokes should occupy the aesthetics section of this treatise. The answer, if unintuitive, is at least simple: because aesthetics deals with the beautiful, and more broadly, what is valued and pleasing, and as jokes are pleasing (wholly because of their capacity for providing pleasure), a joke is in fact an aesthetical project. Understanding why shall unfold the explication of the abovementioned theory.

According to the Contemplation-Comprehension theory, *jokes reveal an unexpected, provocative and pleasure-producing relationship between coherent elements.* Why is this so? To begin with, jokes must be sensible, and their sub-elements plausible. This ensures that a joke is comprehensible and its features identifiable, thereby sparing the audience excessively active efforts in its elucidation (for thought is often strenuous and displeasing). Beyond this cursory feature, the pleasure derived from the actual joke is the result of the audience's *figuring out* the unexpected relationship it contains. This realization produces laughter—that is, expressed pleasure—because in the solution, we discover the unexpected but plausible link, and this variant way of understanding causes us to transition from a state of effortful contemplation (negative utility) to one of realization (neutral utility or positive utility in the solution to a problem and hence egotistic pride), thereby producing pleasure in the closure of this hedonic vacuum (for even the transition from active deliberation to comprehension [while often short of constituting active pleasure] is tantamount to the alleviation of displeasure, and hence, functionally equivalent to active pleasure).[1] Simply, there is a net increase in pleasure, as released by the laughter.

Part of the reason anti-jokes are often humorous is because it takes longer for an audience to understand the relationship between their contained elements, much as their unorthodox formulation and telling produce even larger contemplation-comprehension gaps, of which, when solved, create larger pleasure-producing realizations. This of course assumes that the contemplation-comprehension gap is not so large that it is self-defeating and fundamentally beyond the comprehensibility of the audience.

The merit of any theory which attempts to explain the nature of a subject so quirky and unorthodox as humor might be found more clearly in its capacity to explain related observable phenomena, rather than attempt to rationalize them from afar. Accordingly, we may observe the strength of this theory in its ability to explain the following scenarios:

Repeated jokes are not nearly as funny as their first exhibition, largely because the contemplation-comprehension pattern has already been identified and recalled by the audience. In other words, there is no epistemic gap to fill, and consequently, no hedonic transition from a state of tension to relief. Similarly, rather obvious jokes whose punchlines are easily or preemptively figured out prove unsuccessful because of the inadequate tension rendered by an excessively small hedonic contemplation-comprehension gap. Moreover, with the exception of well-crafted meta- or anti-jokes whose deadpan nature is the source of their comicality, statements of the obvious are not as successful as elaborately contrived scenarios in jokes, for the latter permits a wider hedonic gap to be formed. As a result, the bizarre is often amusing as opposed to the commonplace, for while still

---

1 This understanding, expressed with the emphasis on the resolution of tension, was first advanced by Kant in his *Critique of Judgment.*

similar enough to the banal to be plausible—and hence comprehensible—it is nonetheless far enough removed for active contemplation to be necessary in its understanding. Wordplay and slapstick humor are forms of the selcouth; whereas the former deals with oddities of language, the latter concerns itself with extreme departures from normal and expected physical behavior. Much like with all forms of pleasure, there exists a hierarchy of jokes contingent upon the subtypes of reason to which each principally appeals. The most potent jokes are those requiring the least intuitive reaction; that is, the largest contemplation-comprehension gaps. This is most often achieved through the use of intellectual humor, making use of allusions, references, paradoxes, wordplay, historical incidents (all passive, rote forms of the intellect) and philosophical thinking (the active, more effortful use of the intellect). Contrarily, those jokes reliant upon profanity or crudity usually prove the least durable or successful, for their contemplation-comprehension gaps—and subsequent hedonic transitions—are smallest since comparatively obvious and appeal to the lower subtypes of reason, and hence, the lower pleasures.

PART VII: ECOPOLITICAL UTILISM

Introduction to Retroconservatism

AS PREVIOUS DISCUSSED, Equiist economic and political thought is, ostensibly, divided into theory and practice. Whereas ecopolitical utilism constitutes the latter dimension of this praxis, retroconservatism represents the philosophical underpinnings of our understandings of proper governance and ideal economic exchange. Accordingly, we must begin here, in order to later comprehend its applied tenets.

Retroconservatism is the political philosophy of *Social Naturalism*—the study of human social organization and its underlying mechanisms. Social naturalism, and hence, retroconservatives, advocate that society formed in order to maximize the satisfaction of individual interests, and that for the former to stably thrive, it must accordingly seek to *conserve* its best and necessarily limited resources, of which exist most prominently in the form of human capital. Accordingly, it may be taken as a politically and economically conservative philosophy. Retroconservatism holds reason as its foremost standard in the construction and implementation of public policy. Though it recognizes the historical utility and communitarian bonds afforded by tradition—that is, common morals, history, culture—its valuation is hardly filiopietistic, extending only so far as permitted by its (nonetheless admittedly oft-superior) capacity in serving as a far more potent glue toward optimal social functioning than purely secular or utilitarian politics. This is because while reason ought to serve as our illustrious guide, its edicts are not the sole result of icy logic, but also emotion and the lessons of experience, both of which inform us as to the centrality of common identity, shared values and historical continuity in the stability of the societal unit. While the extent of such traditions need not exceed the negligible, such implies that the optimal size of the social unit is severely limited to the extent that componential subcultures are readily compatible with preexisting norms. Thus, retroconservatism seeks to conserve not tradition so much as the original tool of reason which, originally bare in the natural state of social affairs, is now central to the administration of society. Owing that retroconservatism is based upon the observations of social naturalism, or the natural principles under which humans organize socially, the former recognizes that conservatism as a general political philosophy has long been misunderstood, and a return to its original—and in fact, proper—principles is essential for the continued welfare of society overall.

Freedom is intrinsic and natural, equality not, and to provide for the latter at the cost of the former is as impractical as it is undesirable because unnatural. No trust ought to be invested in a government promising the engineering of human nature. Self-interest, class distinction and parochialism are the inevitable edicts of man, and so should be checked by the State, but never unrealistically repressed. Class stratification is a social necessity; it is the inevitable result of the disparate contributions made by individuals and their relative worth when required to create and maintain a societal unit. The resultant power differential between classes is reflective of the relative worth assigned to each class's respective contribution; this valuation ought to ideally be determined via an objective determination of both the quality and quantity of utility produced, and practically as the result of individual valuations made within a free market. Retroconservatism is a top-down approach to conserve the ideal and limited supply of the best in society—that is, its most productive individuals.

Its tenets are listed below:

> Society is the highest form of human interactional organization—intellectually (through the exchange of ideas), socially, aesthetically, economically, etc. It is true that absolute freedom exists only in a state of nature, but its omnipresent endangerment forces a compromise between individuals so as to form a society, in which each must both give and take. The ideal construction of the body politic therefore, is an arrangement where the greatest possible freedom is afforded to individuals with otherwise-competing interests, thereby approximating the state of nature in all guises except its constant insecurity.

The original anthropological and legitimate purpose of society is to maximize benefit for the individual, not society itself. Prior to the invention of collective goods, such as advocated through religion and other mass symbolic practices, the logic toward social organization emerged from mutual protection and enhanced utility output relative to an anarchic state of nature. Any belief or value system which prioritizes the collective before the individual therefore threatens the original function of society, and must be a practice never state-sanctioned but individually followed. Only broad, minimal public morality initiatives ought to be codified into law, such as the principle of non-aggression and protection from contractual fraud, for such measures are uncontroversial and do not mandate more subjective ethical codes to be respected by the citizenry. Such features ensure maximal individual liberty and conserve the inherence of social naturalism—that people act primarily out of self-interest, and that society serves these interests. By everyone pursuing his own interest, society operates most efficiently overall, because the non-utile are weeded out. This is why society, anthropologically and economically, is not designed to cater for every class of citizen equally, but rather does so in a top-down fashion, valuing firstly the more utilely productive and vital.

This framework translates into permitting significant, unimpeded liberties on the parts of individuals, and minimal governmental intervention—not because liberty is valued as a political right in and of itself, but because it generally promotes enhanced utile output on the part of citizens so inclined to produce. Pursuit of this self-interest maximizes utile efficiency for both its practitioners and the collective community. The State, by virtue of its size and distance removed from personal circumstances shall always possess relatively imperfect information regarding preferences and abilities; for it to more actively interfere in utility production, either by excessive taxation rates or over-regulation of markets, would be to necessarily curb liberties, resulting in economic inefficiencies and utility-diminishment. This same principle extends to legislation which criminalizes self-regarding acts, such as drug use[1] or prostitution, for again, such constitutes a reduction in liberty which violates the only legitimate function of society: to cater to those interests of individuals which do not threaten their peers. Historically, liberal governments prove the most politically illiberal, for in order to enact their utopian schemes, they must almost always necessarily curb individual liberties, through means as diverse as redistributive taxation and surveillance, vigorously using society's most productive individuals as a means to some unachievable egalitarian end. Let us recall that only the rich can afford to be socialists, and in the end, not even them. Contrarily, retroconservatives view the individual only as he naturally exists—as a unit of potential value toward himself and social contribution, services which demand his inherent economic and political respect, both to be taxed commensurate with his consumption of State services,

---

1 Drug use is perfectly moral so long as it increases our pleasure. The self-regarding nature of its usage is irrelevant, for the State may justifiably interfere in this realm if it is reasonably able to promote an individual's welfare better than he can. Because of the intrusiveness and imperfect knowledge possessed by the State, however, such cases are extraordinary, and individual autonomy ought be prioritized. However, the harms predictable from the use of drugs are so great that one cannot reasonably entrust prudence on the part of its consumers; hence, skepticism toward its unobstructed practice must always trump counterclaims of anything less than exceptional proof to the contrary.

and the respect of those rights which ensure his security, from personal privacy[1] to equality before the law.[2]

Society necessitates a division of labor, and the subsequent inequality of the value of such divisions exists by virtue of the relative worth of each type of labor toward society's overall functioning.

The function of government is twofold: to promote social stability, and to defend it; the former is achieved through the guarantee of equality of opportunity, achievable only through minimal intrusions into the otherwise inequality of outcomes characteristic of a free market. Social stability also entails the promotion of public laws. Originally, when societies were homogenous and pre-scientific, this was largely achieved through religious doctrine. Today, because of demographic diversity and the secular eradication of religion, we have reason-based morality whose merit lies in its universal appeal to all rational agents— rather than those with 'divine' or unique access to moral truth. Thus, *conservatism as a political ideology does not concern itself with that which is beyond the purview of reason, the only uncontroversial common denominator in the construction of social rules.* Public laws should promote the good of society through the aforesaid understandings of aesthetics, advocacy for dignified cultural values, and a rejection of obscenity.

It is however important to realize that the public good is occasionally reinforced through traditions of antiquity which, now secular, are harmless—a prime example being constitutional

---

1 Privacy is, again, a utile rule, violable in the interests of a greater good. Its violation is only abhorrent to those made aware of it, and only when regarding themselves. It is only in the natural repugnance toward public knowledge of our affairs that its respect ought be maintained, unless overriding circumstances occur, in which case, it is always best to ensure such intrusions are unknown to their subjects. That said, deception, of any variety, is to be generally disfavored. Few untruths are utile, but too, truth is meaningless if inutile.

2 I can think of no graver utile rule than equality before the law. Exceptionalism permitted in this regard shall be the bellwether of the abuse of privilege by the strong, and the ultimate decline in their respecting obligations to provide deserved resources toward less-enfranchised sectors of the population as part of those larger ends inclusive of the greater good of society which ought be met.

monarchy. Whilst to initiate such a tradition today would be inutile and unjustified, to abolish its representation of historical unity would be equally unjustified in the present.

Not surprisingly, the defense of social stability requires the absence of any form of domestic institutional discrimination (as prejudice in all forms is immoral and inutile, for it differentiates in matters beyond the only acceptable one: merit), though imperialism as a means of cultural diffusion is acceptable so long as it predictably and clearly promotes utility-increasing reforms in its target locale (its proper practice has proven so historically atypical however, that it must first be met by profound skepticism). Moreover, the function of government in the promotion of the public good is to encourage culture—via an aesthetical program as mapped out here, and a respect for quality education, civic instruction in one's social history and the importance of political engagement. Politics should be used to conserve that which is culturally important and stabilizing—including language, culture, cuisine, customs, etc. Religion is an activity which, contrary to reason, should be excluded from State involvement (like all unjustified inutile or unreasonable practices), except in a secular, negligible fashion reminiscent of its preservation of utile traditions (such as monarchy).

Retroconservatism applies the UML on an ecopolitical scale. Equity is achieved through commensurate taxation, whereas benevolence is manifested in those minimal programs toward assisting INAs, such as healthcare for the aged and impoverished, as well as educational access for needy children—especially important since a vital tool in their ultimate empowerment as utility engines. Its absence would guarantee their eventual decline into becoming utility vacuums.

Retroconservatives conserve the liberty and merits of individuals, turning to them first for due treatment, as opposed to unduly benefitting society overall, the expressed goal of liberals. Conservatives seek to conserve the natural condition of social agents as they exist individually. They should only be 'sacrificed,' such as through redistributive taxation, for a distinctly higher good, as to be experienced by a wider number or when the latter's interests are simply overwhelming. Such instances are rare, and their abuse endangers the security of those laws and practices which otherwise protect every citizen's freedoms. Once violated, their repeated violation becomes a more acceptable idea, and hence, only extraordinary instances can bring about exceptionalism as regards the default prioritization of the individual over the collective. The conservation of moral respect for individuals and their liberty is facilitated through flexible government, strong defense, and rigid social penalty for those who threaten legal freedoms. Self-reliance is the engine which makes society productive, and it is this quality which must be encouraged by the government.

Retroconservatives seek a return to the twin reliance of both reason and tradition—seen more as compatible dualities than antagonists—rather than the ever-degenerated and diluted forms modern, and especially liberal, politics has taken, vis-à-vis particularistic agendas, state propaganda, political partisanship, redistributive markets and so on. Retroconservatism is not conservation of tradition beyond what is socially cohesive and thereby utile, but the conservation of the natural condition of man, his reason and its edicts. The actionable manifestation of retroconservatism is ecopolitical utilism, whose origins and tenets are to be expressed forthwith.

Before continuing, we must clarify the denotation of a highly-contested term. What precisely, does it mean to be a 'conservative'? It means not adherence to storied traditions for their own sake, but only if they are utile. It means not a concern for the public morals, unless they catalyze social progress rather than ossify regression. It means not the elevation of one class of citizen over another without reason beyond precedent. No, to be a conservative means to believe that society ought to cater to its best individuals, and that all have the capacity to rise to this category. Conservatives believe the highest virtue which may precipitate both the personal and public good is self-reliance; while praiseworthy for the State to serve toward the most utilitarian ends of society, it is more personally admirable to make oneself such an engine of utility. Before a man ought sacrifice himself for a greater end, he should reform himself so as to be so glorious an end in his own right, and find himself worthy of having others act toward his—and thus ultimately their own—interest. The existence of intrusive government may never permit this eventuality, for the bountiful utility produced by individuals is only the result of their unimpeded labors and the self-reliance encouraged by a minimal state. A conservative asks only that a man produce enough for himself and his dependents, whilst a liberal demands that he produce also for his fellow man. Thus, political conservatism encourages only self-reliance and moral sufficiency, liberalism fosters tranquilizing dependency and mandates excessive charity. Aphoristically, conservatism is a defense of what history has proven works. Fiscal conservatism is, and will always be, a defense of the *status quo* elites—it is a reflection of the most contributory socioeconomic stratification of a society: maximal freedom for the most utile members of society. There is much to be said for the maxim, however incendiary, that productive members of society are always inclined to be conservative.

Notwithstanding this, equality of opportunity is unachievable without at least partial equalization of outcome. The latter is fundamentally counterproductive, and always a temporary solution at best, and hence, must be practiced sparingly. The end result is that there shall always exist within society both unequal opportunity and unequal outcome. And yet, it remains preferable to any alternative state of anarchy. Nevertheless, in the solving of societal woes, there is no solution like that of individual action. Governmental action is the harbinger of the seemingly impossible transformation of lesser problems into worse ones.

Ecopolitical Utilism as Political Practice

Ecopolitical utilism (EU) is similar to classical liberalism, and distinctly named to accentuate its philosophical defense of free markets and individual liberty upon the basis of *utility* as opposed to natural rights or an inviolable respect for personal autonomy. Rights do not exist beyond utile rules, but of the interpersonal realm; duties positively exist however, insofar as they are the product of reason and necessary interdependence upon others. They too do not exist naturally, but only by human contrivance. In brief, EU advocates capitalism with limited welfare provisions and governmental interference as its foremost economic theory, and a democracy led by bureaucratic elites as its political theory. Its economic theory, modeled after the theory of valuation herein expressed as *economic naturalism*, broadly argues that the worth of objects is context-dependent as opposed to intrinsically fixed, and extends only so far as a given good or service possesses the capacity for producing utility under given circumstances.

EU is the result of both theoretical consistency and practical sustainability. Its tenets, as derived from retroconservatism, are derived not only as an extension of meritocratic utilitarianism, but per the realities of what are dynamic though perennially-unequal economic classes within society. It encourages self-reliance on the part of the individual to become a utility engine, whereby resources should *first* be distributed according to utile productivity, and that subsequently, those left remaining, ought to be allocated to the unproductive, involuntarily non-autonomous sectors of society. Of this category, again a utility-hierarchy must prevail. Hence children, who are technically not only an inutile age group, but in fact negatively-utile (for they consume resources rather than produce them), must still be provided for (in this case, presumably by the State if not their own families, since it is the default individual responsibility of able parents to provide first for those dependent upon them by self-device— that is, their decision to bear them), since theirs is a high initial investment but one provably shown to be vital in the continuation of society, and one returned once they become members of the mature, productive generation. The recently-unemployed, possessing a track record of productivity, ought to be allocated those remaining resources within a free-market which might be spent toward their self-improvement, such as through employment agencies and restrained stimulus funding for job growth. Thirdly, we have the elderly, who, in addition to paid-into pension schemes and the like, ought be provided for, considering their prior contributions to the utile functioning of society. The able-bodied homeless should be targeted subsequently, per their potential capacity for government-sponsored or private-sector fostered job programs, the latter often only resultant following government deregulation and lowered taxes. Reticence should be dealt in their treatment, and a general skepticism regarding their capacity for improvement per external agencies, considering their inability or lacked desire to do so by their own hand. Next are the mentally disabled, a truly INA group, followed lastly by the completely unproductive (by choice, not ability), who ought to be provided for minimally in society, and if at all, only out of the intrinsic goodness that is charity insofar as it increases happiness, an innate good, and because it is forgiving of human imperfection (such as sloth), which, because innate to the human character, is desirably pardoned in quantities which do not engender significant cost, such as in this case.

Macroscopically, we can make the connection that the fundamental compensations for talent and labor within retroconservative ecopolitics are broadly equitable, and that in smaller portions charitable action toward INAs is desirable, hence mirroring the interpersonal doctrine of benevolent equity, here applied on a far greater scale. Altogether, its universality produces moral consilience and unification throughout the wide gamut of contextual frames ranging from dyads (the smallest functional unit conducive to moral consideration, since equity is an interpersonal phenomenon) to an entire self-standing free market economy.

The working classes should be given fundamental material comfort, access to affordable healthcare, and education. Education is vital to self-reliance, as is healthcare. The fundamental problem within society is that it does not necessarily value services as it should; for example, the rap 'artist' makes fifty times the college professor. Nevertheless, no government is likely to intervene in changing this, and nor should it be overly quick to try, for the free market is essential in establishing parity levels of value—that is, people earn what others value their services to represent. In this case, such wealth disparity is permissible per the UML in that because of the rap artist's far greater numerical appeal, the sum total of his valued utility exceeds the professor's, even though of an arguably lower quality. Tampering with the free market in general requires excessive intrusiveness and an eventual erosion of freedoms on the part of the government, creating greater inefficiencies in the market than the *status quo*, since the government is incapable of regulating any market of such size competently. It is true that the free market leads to imperfect valuations of labor; but again, to interfere in *any* human system, necessarily imperfect, which has otherwise worked so well, is to almost certainly cause far greater harm. This is especially the case when intervention occurs by a third party incapable of access to information nearly so perfect as that of the market, which respects the individual as the most flexible unit of agency, rather than the sluggish State. Such is why the free market is fundamentally, if not perfectly, just, per the hedonic valuations that its members ascribe not only to individual incomes but also subscribe to via certain services (such as private healthcare, etc.), as based upon the type of private information only individuals have access to regarding personal preferences. Only where rife, destabilizing inequalities, corruption, the threat of monopoly or contractual fraud exists, should the government attempt to intervene. This however, usually has lasting effects, and all government programs/interventions are unlikely to remove themselves voluntarily or surrender their power, so the astute observer ought be critical of this course of action except in extreme situations, of which should virtually always be followed by a swift devolution of the additional, corrective governmental controls introduced. A crisis invariably leads to the metastasis of the State, its growth fueled by the paralysis of fear on the part of the citizenry. Almost never shall be seen a contraction of its power, for it is far simpler to rationalize its continued good on the part of those who benefit most from it, than for them to either relinquish control for fear of its already-corrupting influence, or for the public to act against its abuse before it is too late.

One contemporary problem with politics and political discourse which must be addressed for the success of the aforementioned recommendations is that each political party adopts less-extreme views on matters of public policy and social issues, for centrism is often the most efficacious and reasonable course of action. Such extremism often causes groupthink, bounded rationality and exclusion to thinking more openly about certain ideas, simultaneously promoting party hostility and opportunism on the part of politicians more concerned with survival than promoting the general good. Altogether, these issues further deadlock, often trumping what is utility-maximizing for the society in question. One suggestion is to lessen the incentives for personal gain in politics, such as term limits, reduced salaries, etc. Each carries with it drawbacks, such as either dismissing genuinely-talented politicians forced to end their careers prematurely, or not attracting the best and brightest owing to larger salaries in the private sector. Still, any examination of the current system suggests the likely benefits of seriously considering these recommendations.

A New World Order

In this section, I should attempt to prove that economics, far from being, in the words of Carlyle, that 'dismal science,' is rather a noble yet alienating spirit, cast in realism and pragmatism—an ever so loathed bearer of truth. A discipline dealing with reality and not perfection within the range of the human potential, its goal being the ideal, and not the divine—this is my conception of the power of economics. Herein, I should like to address the economic theory underpinning retroconservative thought so as to put forward a sustainable economic strategy reflective of the realities of the human and social condition. Overall, Equiist economics is best characterized as a compromise between labor exploitation of the lowest socioeconomic classes and the tangible restriction on free enterprise via regulation and taxation, whereby this *wealth-provision/wealth-limitation equilibrium* is essential for the stability of a capitalist state, and whereby economic strife as experienced by the lowest classes is minimized via governmental protections against labor abuse, contractual fraud and deregulation insofar as it permits employment growth and flexibility on the part of the labor force.

Its main theses, and political directives, are as follows:

Ecopolitical Determinism molds the success of any nation's wealth; that is, economics shapes the political structure, which itself determines how resources and wealth may be utilized—itself the determinant of the fate of a nation.

1. Labor exploitation is essential in a capitalist state; otherwise, there can be no provision for material affluence; communist states are inefficient, since without a framework which fosters motivation for success, even if (only theoretically) more equitable in terms of resource distribution. Lower classes are necessary to promote economic efficiency relative to the higher classes; if no such class disparities existed, there would be no impetus afforded by supply and demand incongruities, and the engine of any economy would fall apart. Incentivization would cease, as would technological and social progress and mobility.

2. Fundamentally unregulated capitalism with only restricted welfarist provisions encourages individual productivity while permitting governmental safeguards in exceptional instances for the general population. Competition heightens collective utility by raising standards and augmenting individual efforts.

3. Nationalism is essential to economic prosperity, as is domestic manufacturing and the prioritization of domestic investment over international. Similarly, ideological, as opposed to economically-motivated, foreign interventions usually contravene national interest.

4. Manufacturing and service provision are the most important aspects of preserving a robust economy, for they provide both ample employment opportunities and expansive markets for consumption of their products—both domestically and internationally. Unlike a static industry such as mining, they also promote educational progressivism, and a labor force with evolving skills and specialized knowledge.

5. Globalization inherently weakens a nation's economy (except when it introduces new beneficial technologies or information, or there exists interdependence between strong trade routes for nations [but whereby such are not mercantilistic, involving a rider–horse relationship, forcing one to become dependent upon global networks of trade controlled by another]).

6. Government is operationally optimized by partnership with private enterprise via finite contracts, whereby the latter performs as many of the former's prescribed functions as possible, so long as coincident with the public interest. Government institutions should be held to the

same standards as corporations and allowed to fail if inefficient.

7. Capitalism is the fairest economic theory, in that it provides according to talent and productivity, and hence is a form of economic meritocracy.

On the Normative Foundations of Value and Organization

The purpose of this section, and those which immediately follow, is to shed light on certain economic principles whose merit I have observed both in practice, but more principally, through the application of reason in understanding dynamic economic transactions. In this regard, a normative, rather than positivist, approach has been consistently taken, and it is thus far more the purpose of these findings to lend themselves to theoretical scrutiny than practical application. Primarily, the most novel of conclusions as yet reached involves the requisite imperfection of wealth distribution in any economic system in order to stably preserve the subjectively-perceived value of currency, as well as the necessary exploitation of the lowest classes of workers within an economic organization in order to ensure both maximal production efficiency as well as optimal monetary value. This latter finding would seemingly favor an interventionist policy on the part of governments in the partial regulation of the distribution of wealth, but only so far as taxation and redistribution of non-merit- or non-labor-based transactions of wealth occur, such as inheritance, thereby attempting the greatest possible equality of opportunity by an external force in an inevitably imperfect, somewhat inefficient system. Intervention beyond this point shall inevitably decrease economic efficiency.

The Paradox of Autonomy and Monetary Value Theory

'Every agent in an economic system has the potential to achieve economic freedom and independence, thus producing income superfluous to his summed expenses. This in turn, yields a positive net income. However, though every actor has this assumed ability on the individual, microeconomic level, this ability is neither present on, nor sustainable at, the macroeconomic level.'

The above holds true because of the limitation of resources and capital existent in society insofar as both resources and capital are unable to be equally distributed amongst all economic strata. If such were possible, then this allocation would disrupt the ability of industrial production, since manufacturing efficiency—the sustaining bedrock of stable and self-controllable domestic economic integrity—requires the exploitation of the lowest economic classes (whereby 'classes' shall henceforth refer solely to economic/utility output potential) which inevitably labor to make possible the majority of industrial production power. For an optimally functioning society, there must exist an *ideal* (meaning herein the 'smallest possible amount of an essential and nonzero qualitatively-suboptimal condition,' referring to a situation in which not all can benefit equally or comfortably) inequality between the highest and lowest classes—though namely, this inequality shall emerge most prominently between the middle and lowest classes. Between these, the most disproportionate gap exists in terms of palpable economic exploitation versus labor contributed. This phenomenon, henceforth termed the *Irreducible Class Disparity* (ICD), is epitomized in the case of immigrants who perform menial duties not pursued or practiced by the majority of native-born citizens—the reason being that the 'most undesirable tasks' (defined by the nature and intensity of labor required versus compensation received) are shirked by those whose economic potential permits the freedom to rise above, or avoid, them. This economic potential can only have intrinsic value, and be realized however, in the presence of a less-fortunate economic class whose exploitation must be executed (in their performance of the 'most undesirable tasks'), whereby this class's exploitation is most evident because of their disproportionately large and vital labor contributed toward an organization's economic potential and correspondingly meager income received for such labor.

Hence, a class disparity model, whereby relative distance between classes indicates the increasing degree of exploitation from the 'rich' (assuming that the rich experience zero economic exploitation), would appear roughly as follows:

Rich
Upper-Middle Class

Middle Class
---------------------------ICD------------------------

Working Class

Impoverished Class

The rationale behind such a model is that while the first three classes all have relatively flexible economic potential as determined by their respective abilities to adapt to changing, and especially adverse, economic circumstances, the bottom two classes do not, instead experiencing both highly diminished economic upward mobility and also rigidly fixed and minimal parameters within which to adapt to economic adversity (due to their already limited economic potential and reduced access to those financial autonomy-maximizing tools such as education which make adaptation possible [especially in information economies], or the financial means to acquire them, thus ensuring a vicious cycle of the *status quo*). Of course, the 'impoverished' experience this most forcefully, since members of this class have virtually no means by which to change their economic *status quo* (as they lack the very essential tools for even the slightest change in economic circumstances), and correspondingly are at the mercy of more economically-empowered classes to endure stiffer labor demands for comparatively little economic compensation, a continued form of exploitation which, though exacerbated in times of economic unrest, cannot be pushed too far without horrendous and inutile social consequences brought about by the underclasses.

Moreover, the ICD represents the threshold required in any efficient economic system at which profitable and stable industry shall progress. The reason behind this unpleasant truth is that such inequitable wealth distribution versus labor expended is required in order to give value to money. Thus, *monetary value is the result of unequal monetary distribution, independent of the labor expended by any given economic class.* This is at the core of what shall henceforth be termed *Monetary Value Theory* (MVT).

The theoretical legitimacy of this position can be especially observed when considering its alternative. If every member of society possessed an equal amount of money to the point where he experienced fiscal autonomy, and assuming the money possessed was independent of the labor expended by each individual, then society would no longer remain economically dynamic (a purely fatuous situation however, since individual economic ingenuity would quickly create a stratified class structure anyway). Incentivization would shrivel away for both commercial operations and subsequently, technological innovation. The ripple effect would culminate in nothing less than the immobilization of modern society as we know it. When on the scale of a community, nation-state or global economy, an ICD must exist to allow dynamic economic growth and sector advancement. While economic transitions both holistically and sector-wise are painful, they are the inevitable price of a progress which we remain convinced yields higher utile returns than slavishly remaining fixed to a stable, though suboptimally utile *status quo*.

Hence, MVT states that the value of money is contingent not only upon its supply, but also its distribution amongst the various economic classes. This dispersal, to be known as *stratified equalization*, is crucial in keeping constant the value of money insofar as it remains a mainstay of commercial transactions, as opposed to more objectively agreed upon currencies such as precious metals or commodities. Equally crucial is the required physical supply of money to adequately permeate each of the classes to a degree which neither artificially deflates nor inflates its value, but which, together with stratified equalization, determines and keeps relatively constant the *perceived value* (VP) of money within a given economic system.

When extended, this view would advocate a sense of *economic naturalism*, whereby the macroscopic success of an economy depends upon dynamic competition and the inevitable profit and loss had by individual parties, and collectively, respective classes. More specifically, it necessitates a pyramidal economic

The End of Knowledge

structure, whereby the highest economic classes are fated to remain the most profiteering and simultaneously the least industrious overall, likely due to their inferior numbers. Their profit capacity is the result of the quality of their talents as perceived within free market valuations, not its quantitative generative capacity. Take for instance the idea that the multimillion dollar annual salaries of CEOs are instead salaries more equitably deserved by those working hardest and most meaningfully toward producing objects/services not of VP, but rather of *intrinsic value* (VI), whereby the latter is defined as an object/service's 'required amount of labor and the utility, or functional value, as determined by situational demands rather than objective criteria, of said object/service to consumers as compared to similar other objects/services.' Though this definition cannot entirely rid itself of subjective valuation, it nonetheless is better able to illustrate the more objective value of a blacksmith to society *in economic terms* than a surrealist painter. If one assumes that multimillion dollar salaries should be directed toward those who most meaningfully contribute toward VI objects and services within society, then one must elevate these individuals and classes to the higher levels of the economic pyramid. Thus, if a CEO does comparatively little to produce VI as opposed to a schoolteacher who empowers his students with the skill base necessary to earn a future living, the latter must switch places with the former in the economic hierarchy. Thus, the amount of money within the system would remain constant; it would only be redistributed to different individuals and classes.

While this may seem like a prudent, perhaps even morally compelling position, it is a flawed one nevertheless. The CEO-schoolteacher example illustrates a utility/income disparity which is *required* on a macroscopic level in the most economically efficient system. This is because exploitation (thus defined as receiving a lower income relative to higher VI production capacity) must always occur amongst the industrial, laboring majority, for it is this segment of the population which, most superior in number, is required to manufacture cheap products or provide inexpensive services for consumption. The alternative would be that the majority would be spending too much on needed items/ services, thus artificially raising the price of non-unique and abundant products/services. This phenomenon is known as the *Principle of Suppressed Intrinsic Value*, because it argues that products and industrial processes would become too expensive if not for requisite cheap mass labor sources, which are the engines of efficient and widespread corporate competition and subsequent innovation and cost-reduction for the consumer, resulting in overall optimal economic system efficiency. A corollary of this principle would suggest that by virtue of the population numbers required for optimal VI production, the highest classes must have the highest income and lowest VI.

Without some degree of the economic exploitation outlined above, money loses its status as an item valued in and of itself, and hence its incentivizing mechanism to encourage economic growth and prevent stagnation, much as it partially forfeits its status as a potent symbolic commodity of common meaning and value in bartering transactions. Moreover, when examining the nature of potential microeconomic autonomy versus actual macroeconomic class polarization, we can conjecture that if each member of society were fiscally autonomous, the concept of financial autonomy would lose all worthwhile meaning, since economic leverage in the form of class/buying disparity would give way from a once-ideal mutual interdependence model to an outright reliance upon others' services—but in this latter case, a reliance marked *by no common means of transactional bargaining*, since money becomes valueless. The most extreme form of this economic anarchy would be the realization of the redundancy of society as a solely economic organization. Thus, it is reaffirmed that some inequity is crucial for the overall functioning of a macroeconomic system, for the dystopian alternative of an egalitarian arrangement is sure to be marked by total systemic failure. It is a fine balancing act to ensure optimal efficiency through minimal inequality.

There is another angle by which to approach the Paradox of Autonomy. Recall that individuals within the majority are further incapable of pure autonomy because no universal access to all vital resources required for such economic autonomy exists for any individual. This of course reiterates the mutual interdependency by which society is made economically dynamic, and encourages that once trading occurs for valued commodities, transactions between parties will ensure an upset in wealth. This in turn would ultimately result in the inevitable benefit of certain parties over others (since perfect symbiotic benefit is, though possible in the immediate present, impossible to sustain), yet preserve the integrity of the system as a whole.

The Principle of Scarcity-Induced Value

'Limitation, either natural or anthropogenically-engineered, of desired resources or currency, maintains such items' value, because there exists a subsequent incentive to acquire each because of their inadequate supply to accommodate seemingly limitless demands. Alternatively, ample supply of a desired item drives down its transactional value. Thus, there is an inverse relationship between supply and demand, whereby the latter does not change by itself, but rather in response to a change in supply. Utility is not a criterion of demand so much as supply.'

Competition within an economic system ensures the continued valuing of money and resources, because there is a constant risk that their value may diminish or increase, thus driving the desire to continually augment one's supply of them (either as insurance against their devaluation, since more of good X is now required to maintain parity, or to maximize profit should X become more valuable). The demand for increasingly-greater supply can be represented by a negative exponential graph, where supply is the independent variable. Conversely, when not in possession of money and/or resources, there is an ever-present demand which spurs action to obtain them. If this economic-psychological reality did not exist, then the value of an item would be divorced from its abundance, and inevitably devalued transactionally.

While it may seem intuitive that demand drives supply, it is misguided to consider supply subsequent to demand because such a scenario is both inefficient and less profitable on the supply-side (which holds an unequal position of greater power due to its unique manufacturing/production ability) to the alternative (whereby demand is subsequent to supply), and assumes a teleological or purposeful awareness to be at work in demand formulation. Rather, the demand-supply interplay is better likened to natural selection, in which a set of random variations in the form of various suppliers available present themselves for demand, and demand is determined based on the available supplies. Following this understanding, it is only reasonable to conclude that scarcity is the criterion for assigning value. Excluding extreme instances where disparities in utility become the overarching factor, sufficient utility is present in the vast majority of items so that utility no longer becomes the dominant factor in the assignment of value (as represented by an item's monetary price), but rather, its supply, since an almost always excessive demand will exist for any relatively scarce item (fur coats, expensive sports cars, Pollock paint drips, a hand-sewn rhinestone cape, mother-of-pearl seashells, etc.). This comes partly because of the perception that value is legitimized subsequent to exclusivity, and that what is openly available no longer retains its status as an item of value, since prestige is a function of rarity. More importantly however, this understanding sheds new light on the idea that demand is crafted subsequent to supply, since those with the potential for production and manufacturing/catering of services [the supply-side] will remain economically incentivized to engineer demand to their own advantage with the resources most easily available to them, rather than tailoring their efforts to conform to popular demands. One possible perversion of this awareness would be the tendency for supply-side producers to falsify the scarcity of an otherwise-abundant commodity easily available and producible by themselves, in an attempt to maximize profits and minimize production costs (especially when a high demand for it is predictable or currently demonstrated [e.g., petroleum price gouging after a hurricane, where higher fuel prices *simulate* the functionalist result of increased demand, despite there being no actual decrease in supply]), though it is unlikely to remain a sustainable practice since public awareness of this item's apparent non-scarcity over time would drive demand—and hence prices—down.

In its most conservative form, this principle argues that when utility remains constant, it is supply which drives demand, especially since it remains economically advisable for the supply-side to not perfectly cater in a 1:1 ratio with demand, but rather force a limited supply to increase demand, thereby maximizing profits. While this is an unsustainable practice per item, it is likely to occur over supply rising to meet demand perfectly, since this is less immediately economically profitable (and hence likely disdained over a more immediately profitable alternative), and because this practice of supply driving demand can simply be reincarnated with a new item/resource/fad displacing the current trend, as opposed to resorting to a more long-term supply-meeting-demand approach. On the demand-side, it is psychology which fuels this phenomenon rather than short-term economic pragmatism: value is a function of perceived exclusivity, oftentimes regardless of utility. Overall, competitive demand for what is in low supply maximizes short-term efficiency to obtain such resources on demand-side, though it is important to note once again that such efficiency maximization may lead to unsustainable long-term practices.

The Theorem of Valuation

'Value is determined through constant attention to the need for a product or available service—either by lacking it or being aware of the risk of losing it and hence seeking to prevent this outcome. Inattention to the aforesaid because a product is perceived to be non-useful, non-prestigious or already possessed and not required in greater supply, nor at risk for being lost, in whole or in part, invariably devalues said product or available service.'

When either through lack of utility or engineered demand via supply, inattention to the significance or need for a given product lessens the acuteness of its demand, and hence, value, much as heightened attention toward a product/service raises its transactional value. Thus, much as the Principle of Scarcity-Induced Value requires focused attention to the current scarcity of a good (thus elevating its demand), so too is value to a much broader extent a function of attention in general—where admittedly, this attention can, unique to the good in question, be in response to either its utility, engineered demand via supply or adequate supply.

Unification So Far

What is the remarkable progress we have made thus far? We have constructed a theoretical framework internally consistent and unified at multiple levels. We have learnt that reason is at the ultimate core of understanding all phenomena across virtually every discipline by way of epistemic commensurability, including serving as even the ideal instrument by which to form judgments and live life. We have unified Equiist aesthetics and politics as a direct extension of its ethics, the latter pair centered upon the principles of merit and benevolent equity. Ethics itself has been revolutionized within our framework, transformed from a contested and irreconcilable discipline to one of concatenating concinnity across formerly-incompatible schools of thought. For, as has been shown, all moral frameworks ultimately collapse into understandings of preference satisfaction: utile rules for deontology, explicit calculation for utilitarian theories themselves, and personality traits in virtue ethics which represent a shorthand for utile potential based upon the likely behavioral patterns and outputs of men. It is our greatest achievement thus far in the history of moral philosophy—the unification of the ancient and modern, of theories focused on character and action, their intents and motivations, from the fusing together of stoic thought and hedonic flair, deontological awe for the individual and consequentialist logic in the face of untenable omission to act. Altogether, we have crafted a science of the due, not just in terms of moral and political fairness, but epistemic properness. We have stressed that political practice must be consistent with prescribed moral practice, and pass the ultimate test of dual legitimacy: philosophical rigor and universal actionability, requisitely compatible within the universalizable moral frameworks presented, such as BE, MU and their broader manifestation as ecopolitical utilism.

If, at this point, my ethics were to be forcibly reduced, I would say this: its vital elements include the primacy of pleasure as a criterion of moral behavior, the necessity of actions equitable in intent and magnitude, and the praiseworthiness of charity. Moreover, it recognizes that pleasures, like people, are not equal, as much per their talents as their individual choices, and accordingly, prioritizes the moral rights of the most beneficially impactful, per their capacity for the effectuation of firstly the most superior pleasures to be then experienced by the greatest number of worthy agents, whereby desert is defined per both the scale of one's potential hedonic output and the nature of his moral character. Only in times where the greater deserving would be compromised may an unjust man be rewarded for actions which, if ignored, would harm the greater good. Such of course, is a manner of last resort. Equiism is the systematic guide to living a good life. It recognizes the supreme respect which must be paid the individual, but also the overarching priority which must be given society in extraordinary instances, in which the worth of individuals is directly proportional to their proven and potential utility. It relies upon reason to provide us the ceaseless opportunity for self-willed happiness, of which is only possible via moral behavior—itself a combination of justice and benevolence.

PART VIII: BEING HAPPY

NOT LONG AGO, I wrote that simple words are noblest. I have not changed my mind, and hence, in this, most important section, shall commit myself to that belief. I am a young man, who, despite the blessings of sound upbringing and definite wisdom beyond his years, is one nevertheless far less experienced in the matters of the world—both good and bad—than many of those who share with me this rich reality called life. Accordingly, I should not profess my views, collectively or piecemeal, to be sacrosanct, nor to be followed by anyone other than those who independently come to find their offerings worthy of adherence. Still, I cannot tell an untruth; as far as I am concerned, I have completed an essential project in my life—I have defined my values, and the means by which in attaining them I may find satisfaction. I have decided to make happiness my life's work, and to that end, I should like to record by what means I hope to achieve that goal. I have lived for one purpose, and one alone: to be happy, and live with the knowledge I am worthy of it.

For me, the answers, now in retrospect, prove remarkably simple, and yet, required years of anguished toil in their discovery. Perhaps this is the cruel irony of fate—that our greatest, simplest, truths, emerge only after intense deliberations and varied experiences. The greatest truths are always simple by necessity—alas, their discovery, never so. The deepest truths cannot be known and followed simultaneous to analytic scrutiny—they exist pure, action-guiding and compelling wholly on their own. They may only be recognized wholly—via the intellect, emotion and experience—and embodied accordingly. While it is impossible to lay down on paper all these verities I have identified as important in the living of the good life, it is nevertheless important to reaffirm that it is more important to be sure in our minds, hearts and actions, than it is to be on the page. I do not seek fame or posterity, so much as I do joy in this, my one, life. A man contented not in life but posterity is worthy of neither. For me, philosophy has provided that open route, made possible by its directing me toward the highest of all earthbound purposes— the embodiment of reason in pursuit of crafting the most ideal judgments within life. Only philosophy rises to meet this divine function, and in so doing, remains defender of the possibilities of our highest potential.

I have reduced life to a series of simple propositions and objectives which must be completed for its fullest enjoyment. Doing so was by no means effortless, but identifying what must be done, I have found, now is. For me, the entirety of the good life can be reduced to an unflinching, omnipresent obedience to reason. Its dictates are universal, their explication general, and their sufficient enactment always possible. And of course, by reason I do not mean pure and blind rationality, but those methods of action and judgment which, most reflective of our nature—the logical, the emotional and the learnt from experience—relate themselves in the ideal enjoyment of life. I mean, quite simply, that which is required in being, 'a reasonable man.' This includes following a simple formula: following our effortless intuition except when overt rationality dictates its own use for prudence's sake in unfamiliar territory, not fearing to sublimate rationality into emotional impulses when required for our greater and merited happiness, and being guided by the untranslatable knowledge of experience when neither rationality nor emotion proves wholly successful. That these procedures, in addition to the occasional and *ultimate* corroborating check (owing to its impartial consistency) of rational analysis, are used to both discern the best route before us in any matter, and to intermittently ensure ours is a fundamentally moral character, and whereby if not, that sufficient correction is subsequently made. Unity is strength, as much within oneself between mind, body and principle, as with each other through care and consideration. There is no prescriptive or precise formula which yields this concoction; it is forged in the magic crucible afforded by wisdom and its pursuit. The secret to being happy is simple and as follows: we must, within reason, and as ought all things be pursued, ceaselessly self-improve with the ambition of fulfilling our utmost potential, and hence maximize our capacity for hedonic experience, to experience the highest and widest variety of pleasures, and to seek no more than that which we cannot change reasonably—or whereby to pursue such wants would require greater effort or pain than the likely pleasure received. Life is ever-navigable if we wish it to be, and ever so that such ease may coincide with virtue, so long as its pursuit is governed by reason. When once asked how I would define this elusive concept, I replied that happiness is being satisfied with who one is, when all alone at day's end. To be happy one need never look beyond himself, nor be tempted by the exigencies of public renown. Greatness cannot ever come at the price of wickedness. Rather, it is the alignment of large consequence and moral character. It is the result of natural capacity and willful choice, scarcely fleeting, but the attribute of unchanging character. Accordingly, happiness is a project of self-reliance, whose experience is ultimately, inevitably, always private, and not the fodder of desperately sought-after notoriety. And, to this end, envy no other—you know not his hidden reality. Rather, make what is good in his life your own. Who then, is a great man? It is he who sacrifices everything for his moral purpose, and is deterred not in the slightest if done in utter anonymity.

The totality of the struggle between good and evil is remarkably simple to understand, and may be defined by two axes: propinquity and courage. Want is the root of all good as much the root of all evil. The difference in its effects stems from the direction of our desire—to be worthy of happiness through moral obedience, or to pursue unabashed self-interest at the expense of others. My advice is to therefore live today as you would remember tomorrow. It is this prospective retrospection which mandates our obedience to morality, for cognizant of our future being, no short-term gain brought about at the cost of inequity may compare to the enduring blissfulness associated only with the absence of guilt. To embody goodness requires the endurance of hardship in return for deep, durable pleasure at the cost of possible short-term gain, whereas evil sacrifices sustained desert in favor for immediate, ill-gotten pleasure. The sufficient discipline to pursue the former requires a sense of courage absent from the latter. Courage to obey the moral duties of reason, often against our immediate self-interest—that is the price of happiness, and not an unfair one, for at birth, we are deserving of neither joy nor sorrow, and it is only through labors, through moral activity, that we may call ourselves worthy of pleasure. Morality is but the means to the end of happiness.

To be a good, happy and wise man—each quality, when true, the result of the presence of the others—is not painless, but not ever so arduous that it requires us to behave unreasonably. There is no conflict within unconquerable by reason. In reason lives our moral ideal—stretching from virtuous fundamentality to excellence. And because of the accessibility of these virtues and their enjoyment requiring nothing more than a will composed not of extreme but commonplace strength, therein too lays its absoluteness in defining a moral threshold which clearly separates good from evil men. These distinctions exist in moral objectivity, which, however difficult to sense by men, appeal strongly enough to our senses and reason to be adhered to fundamentally and sufficiently. Few men have the capacity for excellence, but all possess the capacity for adequacy. It is vital to realize that the path of reason is always before us, providing the ever-present opportunity to experience happiness, itself wholly our responsibility to enjoy. This is not to paint a naïve picture of life as one in which inner-satisfaction cannot be significantly affected by those around us or external circumstances, but I do assert that with courage and the cultivation of discipline we can close ourselves off from the harm of externality, instead only becoming dependent upon others when likely to augment our pleasures, not forgetting to reciprocate their beneficial labors when so necessary.

Nothing requires greater courage than to be happy. This stoic flavor of Equiism is essential in maintaining self-reliance throughout life, and ensuring that that which exists beyond the powers of our will should not be considered important to our contentment. The stoic element of Equiism stresses that we firstly limitlessly seek happiness, understanding that its boundless experience cannot ever be harmful or destabilizing, that only in unavoidable sorrow must we accept what cannot be changed and make the best of it, and to appreciate all events in our life in the appropriate perspective. In this capacity, thus does Equiism advocate a unique, 'one-way' stoicism: the boundless pursuit of the pleasing in one direction, and an immediate stop-valve to unalterable sorrow through toleration rid of all lingering emotional attachment. Such invincibility is possible, but only through the most cultivated sense of discipline and the will. Life is difficult, and no staged adaptation exists so effectively as the shock treatment of self-reliance in the enduring cure of its ills. That while happiness cannot come without ceaseless self-improvement and the accompanying ambitious desire to do so, true joy cannot come short of our acceptance of those imperfections whose eradication proves far costlier than the benefits of their presence, much less acceptance of those events beyond our powers to control. I find every challenging period of my life but an opportunity to savor its hidden pleasures all the more. Joy and sorrow are therefore dependent not on circumstance but choice.

Every struggle before me I insist on converting into indulgence, far more so than I would if otherwise unimpeded. Who then, is the enemy within? It is the most insidious villain of all: bitterness in the face of opposition. Defeat is not so great an evil as despondency, for it is one misfortune, universal to all, to be pummeled by the fists of outsiders, but a greater horror to offer yourself to them by virtue of surrender or submission. Such is to become a slave to circumstance, not a master of self-determination. So long as one possesses the will to live and be happy, one must never resign himself to sullenness, but an ever-present determination to find happiness in the darkest of hours, and to pave the avenue of future luminance. To be ever exerting of one's will toward self-betterment and improved circumstance is not optimism—the unfounded search for such better circumstances—but the highest form of ambition, the refusal to allow others to dictate one's life path or its quality. It is defiance of the noblest form. Let us not be swayed thus by optimism nor pessimism—but only realism and the inexhaustible potentiality of our being.

The importance of our emotional character is emphasized as regards the paralysis of terror. We cannot think nearly as well as act out of the clutches of fear, most often spurred at the heels by instinct to soldier forwards, even in the face of uncertainty and anguish. For, the former requires a form of intellectual perfection not readily achievable in order to dispel a fear; it demands of us to not only rationalize away the illegitimacy of our trepidations, but to recall such logic without interruption, requiring conscious thought of all that which defuses a fear once prompted. Rather, to live through a fear and emerge intact, intrinsically defangs its dread, with no effortful analysis—it is not that our fear is defused each time discredited by the intellect, but due the intuitive memory of experience. Fear is only unconquerable before it is conquered.

Our goal ought not to be the impossibility of perfect happiness, but rather joy as a permanent, durable condition—so much so that melancholy is but an aberration, mercilessly challenged and expunged as soon as its presence is known. In this sense, we possess the dual advantage of savoring the pleasures afforded us without constraint or limit, consciously taking no available joy for granted, regimenting stoic restraint only when necessary to shield ourselves from its unfortunate elusion. Perfection as conflated with greatness is a familiar err, pardoning not the one who chooses 'greatness' of this ilk over happiness, and who necessarily forfeits both. The former is a phenomenon valued only by others, the latter, by ourselves—the only bearers to whom our experience matters. We are the ones solely responsible for our happiness. The greatest bafflement is that most view living well secondary to the demands of the mere exigencies of the present—education, profession, posterity, wealth, status—none of which is at the root of true satisfaction. How too few of us have made pursuit of happiness our highest priority! Rarer still than traditional genius—the life of torment, of intensity, the lust for greatness obnubilated by irrational guilt in the face of inevitable imperfection—is the mastery of knowledge of how to live well.

For this, an even higher breed of intelligence and intrepidity is required. It appears one of the greatest paradoxes of life that the vast majority, including most of the brilliant men in the world, fail to prioritize the quality of their lives as worthy of effort in and of itself. That professional achievement or social advancement requires our unwavering attention and dedication, but not the building of our own happiness and pursuit of beauty—is perhaps the greatest illusion of all time, and one swallowed by almost everyone.

Hence, unification occurs on yet another level, in recognizing that hedonism and stoicism are hardly incompatible, but that the latter is necessary in durably pursuing and maintaining the former. The discipline required to do this, and to realize that only through moral behavior may we be happy, comes not at once, but through trial and hardship, reflection and improvement. But, for the man dedicated to courage, such pained transitions shall prove fleeting rather than protracted, allowing him to breathe freely that much sooner with a moral purpose in his life. Every temptation which jeopardizes moral fundamentality can be toppled with courage motivated by reason and thus confident in its moral integrity. For, there is nothing more tempting than the prospect of deserving to enjoy existence. How many more men may be happy from such advice, yet fail to prioritize living a worthwhile life? How many possess the potential, but lack the courage of will? Happiness is not prejudiced, but neither generous; its mastery comes only if made our highest concern. And, toward this end, I serve only reason in its pursuit.

Pride is the mother of all joy; fear, the mother of all pain. For pride requires us to seek the sating of our ego, interpersonally and intrapersonally, the latter being the result of personal desire. Only in our valuing ourselves through pride do we identify the value in life to be sought out—from the corporeal to the satisfaction of moral obligation. Contrarily, all pain is the result of fear: guilt, the moral fear of unworthiness of happiness, embarrassment, the fear of social ostracism, loss, the fear of the future absence of some source of past happiness, uncertainty, a fear of the unknown. There are few absolutes in life; 'tis too true that truths are cast only in halves. But among them, are included the following: that happiness is the only good; that its realization cannot be fullest without others; and that morality is therefore required in its social desert. So, while it can never all be said, thought or figured out—we may come close enough.

Altogether, the successful operation, transition between, and overlapping of the aforementioned components of reason lead to pursuit and attainment of more than one end. Firstly, they are all intrinsically governed by our innate gravitation toward pleasure, accordingly, the only undisputed good. Second, and more important, they compel us toward moral behavior—those actions which allocate effortful happiness-producing resources toward those most worthy of them, including, if so deserving, ourselves. To this end, we are further compelled to obey the commandments of equity and benevolence—the twin pillars of all morality. We are to know that justice is the highest priority of our actions, but to not dismiss the importance of charity, recognized as its own good in the provision of pleasure, and also its forgiveness of those imperfections which typify what it means to be human. For, in the forgiveness of others, so too may they, and we, forgive ourselves. The happy man is one who, through reason, comes to behave morally, for his own happiness must emerge from knowledge of his desert for it—a worthiness which is only carried through moral behavior. In this very simple sense, happiness is knowing one deserves it. Its price: the courage to act reasonably and morally. Just as others aid us in being happy through their labors, characters and love, we must reciprocate, for we are otherwise cheating them of their due compensation. Failure to do this inevitably leads to a man's recognition of his unworthiness of happiness, which cannot be enjoyed without a prerequisite knowledge of its desert. Only moral behavior can ensure this prerequisite knowledge, and the only man immune from this requirement is he who lives alone in the wilderness, incapable of equity because he has no one else with whom to behave equitably, much as he cannot experience happiness in its highest forms since starved of the intellectual and emotional species borne only through social intercourse. From reason as wisdom stems moral behavior from which stems happiness. Thus, reason, moral being, and pleasure are all inextricably intertwined.

Ensuring that one dedicates his labors to the cause of his

own self-justice and that of worthy others, and venturing to behave at times magnanimously, are the keys to happiness. Just as
Nietzsche had his will to power, Freud his will to pleasure and
Frankl his will to meaning, herein I pronounce my *will to rightness*—that the thinking man cannot live fully without making
his a life of moral principle, recognizing that pure happiness exists not in its enjoyment as much as its prior desert, whereby the
accompanying knowledge of such worthiness is itself the highest and most enduring form of satisfaction, for it appeals to the
universal, uncompromising nature of its object of study.

This is not to discount the importance of self-improvement,
of which must follow from ambition. This feature of the happy
man is vital as it permits him to explore those new activities
whose mastery shall diversify not only the pleasures of his own
life, but make richer his capacity to better the lots of others. In
this pursuit of ever-betterment, we cannot forget that by virtue of our human limitations, we may never attain, and hence
should not aspire toward, perfection. There is nothing so insidi-
ously self-destructive as its pursuit. We must embrace that extent of our morality which is most compatible with reason and
happiness—a threshold which shall always be compatible with
the character of a good man. Morality shall never require us to
endure extremes, for its less virtuous alternatives shall be more
crushing to our capacity for happiness. Learning is a difficult
process, whose lessons are seldom kept with simultaneity in
our mind, but whose reassurances exist dually after much hardship, and appear often in fleeting moments of reflection, rather
than an ever-watchful sentinel ensuring flawless judgment. We
must often venture forward from our present knowns in order to
grow, carefully balancing the prudence of past wisdoms yet not
fearing to expand to new dimensions of perfecting that which
we desire, so as to perfect the quality of our behaviors, experiences and knowledge. Because there exist no utopias or Experience Machines within the realm of man, in a stoic attitude do we
find the surest means of minimizing the inevitable slings of dis-
appointment and rather forge the adamantine resolve to become
ever more immune to their wounds. For, while it is not ideal to
endure pain so as to value the pleasing, it appears necessary in
reality, and further urges that not a single moment ought to be

wasted in pursuit of the most halcyon experiences available to us. And so, be sure not to make reason's pursuit its own extreme, but rather the shadowed yet guiding principle of our life. That it be reflected upon periodically, and its edicts measured relative to their fundamental success or failure, and adapted appropriately, are sufficient to lead a morally satisfactory and contented life. No aporia thrives so well that one cannot know ultimately how to morally overcome it.

Being happy is not a difficult goal to understand, but certainly one to attain. It is not had without conscious effort, and requires ever-new conviction and boundless courage to once more seize every time it eludes us with shattering heartbreak. Because attitude is the prism by which our worldview is framed, applying our will toward coloring the rosiest lens is vital if we are to take the quality of our life seriously. Neither judgment by others nor external sources of validation can match the sincerity and durability of personal integrity in prioritizing and judging our conscience. Above all my realizations regarding its taming, none has stood more indestructibly than its inextricable relationship with moral desert, and that to this end, nothing but our self-fixed attitude is necessary in its creation. Nothing beyond the will need be relied upon in order to bask in the sunniest of delights, but the self-knowledge and capacity to do what is right for others and oneself. Such are the fruits of the proper auscultation of the conscience. The alternative is a life of guilty regret, and one always foreseeable at the time of its birth. Only the cowardly and stupid could accept such a fate where short-term convenience trumps long-term satisfaction. This is not to fatuously claim that regret may never be encountered; a life without regret is a life not lived at all. Regret then, only those decisions which were regrettable at the moment of inception. The regret of hindsight is as futile as it is unjustified. While life may be beautiful, such bounties do not come without discipline and the effortful application of reason, of stoicism and actively appreciating all the pleasures before us and too often ignored. Show me a man discontent with his lot, and more often than not he should be one blind to exploitable joys before him. To seek happiness with unrelenting fervor, of the highest and widest variety—that should be the clarion call to all men. We ought to do this because we must be moral in order to deserve it, itself recognized as the highest good we mortals may attain. We ought do this because through perfecting our moral constitution do we in fact augment our worthiness of greater happiness, as a more valued utility provider, for others and toward ourselves, for the most morally important man is he who leads the happiest life, both due his beneficial impact upon others as much the wondrous existence he personally leads.

I do not have all the answers, nor ever will—and I am content with that ignorance, for it falls within that inevitable inability of mine to embody perfection. It cannot all be said or known, but it is in the glory of trying and ever-nearing these twinned goals wherein lies the glory of man. Close enough may we always reach our aims (their wholeness known, intuitive and distinct, ever-more real in practice and the soul that is reason and the source of our dignity, domiciled in the mind, than the bland page or isolated thought), that we may be judged—and that is a truth sufficient enough to live by with the aim of being a good man, whose life ought ever be a vessel for happiness pursued. Life may not ever be distilled wholly into a sentence, treatise or philosophy, however close personal judgment and analysis may come. To accept that mysterious gap of knowledge is itself one of the wonders which provides us renewed adventure and a desire to continue creating and self-defining our purpose. It is in the vagaries of human judgment, in its imprecision, which lies the glory of wonder, the acceptance of imperfection, the recognition of our nature, and ultimately, the permission to experience ceaseless happiness. The very purpose and value of meditation is to elevate oneself beyond the reach of earthly pain and enjoy the richer pleasures of a higher consciousness fertile in laying claim to these discoveries.

To ask, 'what is the meaning of life?' I have learnt, is the wrong question, for there is no prescription in the stars, but in the mind and the heart. Instead, we must question 'what is the highest goal of life?' And to that, I say that I have found my truth. I believe that while our meaning is self-defined, such is untroubling since the absurdity of the universe around us means little if otherwise uninvolved in our lives. I reject the absurd and the despair—because I can. I define my existential purpose as not one conducive to subjective whim or without merit relative to others', but one of objective prescription and superiority. For me, it is that the meaning of life is to be happy—through pursuit of individual pleasure and its personal moral desert—and making worthy others so. That the highest personal meaning divinable is to dedicate oneself to the embodiment of morality, and hence, personal happiness. That happiness is and follows from virtue, itself the fruit of reason. To deserve happiness is the prerequisite to all of its subsequent offspring, and, while not sufficient for sustaining existence by itself, is the necessary condition, the most important, and the highest singular form of bliss. And so, there is no higher calling than the one before us all—our highest purpose, our omnipresent capacity, our self-deserved duty—yet one nonetheless taken up by too few, and too late, the result of lacked courage as much as inattentive reflection. Above all, *dare to be happy!*